A Career Guide for Physician Executives

2nd Edition of
Hope for the Future

by Barbara J. Linney, MA

American College of Physician Executives
4890 West Kennedy Boulevard, Suite 200
Tampa, Florida 33609-2575
813-287-2000

ISBN: 0-924674-98-9

Library of Congress Card Number: 2006924323

Printed in the United States of America by Lightning Source, Inc., St. Louis, Missouri.

Preface

I have a theory, warmed by experience even though unsubstantiated by hard evidence, that almost every physician now plowing the management fields will find him- or herself unemployed at least once in the years ahead. Just as likely, I think, each physician executive will find it necessary to reinvent him- or herself and locate new opportunities in a health care field that is under constant change.

The race in all this will go to the swift and the flexible—to those who can anticipate changes in the structure and hiring needs of the health care field and respond to them aggressively. Those wedded to the status quo will find it difficult to survive in medicine and impossible to survive in medical management. Even many swift and flexible souls will struggle in an environment characterized by intense competition. Health care organizations will be battling for customers, and their managers will be asked on a regular basis to show what they've done for the organization lately.

But there will continue to be places for persons who can operate at the edge of the marriage between medicine and management. It is unlikely that the purpose of health care, the entrepreneurial noises of some notwithstanding, will ever be other than the provision of health care services. And the person who understands the nuances of health care delivery can expect a place, a significant place, in the health care delivery world.

That place will have to be won, however; it will not be given. This book, I think, shows how to prosper if your chosen profession is medical management. There are reasons for optimism, but there are also reasons to prepare for the very different employment world ahead.

Roger Schenke
Executive Vice President
American College of Physician Executives
October 1996

About the Author

Barbara J. Linney is Vice President of Career Development for the American College of Physician Executives. She is recognized nationally for her work in career counseling, management development, and communications training. Barbara's successful background includes one-on-one counseling in organizational and interpersonal skills, seminar presentations, articles published in health care and management periodicals, and college-level teaching.

Ms. Linney is a graduate of Westhampton College, Richmond, Virginia; earned her master's degree from the University of North Carolina-Charlotte; and has completed coursework for a doctorate from the University of South Florida, Tampa.

Introduction

The following quote was in a book called Crisis Proof Your Career. "'This is a test....This is only a test. Had this been your real life, you would have been shown where to go and what to do."[1] This sarcastic jolt reminds us—this is my one and only life, and I won't be given a set of instructions. I have to figure out what I want to do. Effective, happy people make those decisions for themselves, but it takes time. You must sit still, be reflective, figure out what you want and how to get it. No process guarantees that you will get everything you want, but many have reported that they feel a sense of meaning in their lives, some direction from a higher power, when they have taken the time to reflect and plan. "The goal...is to create...a plan—one that is loose enough for providence to intervene and tight enough to keep...on course month by month."[2]

In these turbulent times for health care, we wanted in this book to offer you a guide for making career plans for yourself whether you move toward medical management, stay in clinical practice, or leave medicine altogether.

Chapter 1 describes the types of physician executive jobs people in the know are predicting for the future. Chapters 2, 3, and 4 will help you examine your professional and personal lives and prepare for change. Chapter 5 discusses how to get the experience that organizations and recruiters want you to have. Chapter 6 discusses communication skills needed for success. Chapters 7, 8, and 9 describe the "get down and dirty" skills of getting a job—networking, resumes, and interviews. Chapter 10 has advice for negotiating salaries. Chapter 11 tells how to cope with getting fired. Finally, Chapter 12 suggests some tools to use throughout the job search process.

Viktor Frankl wrote in Man's Search for Meaning, "Life ultimately means taking the responsibility to find the right answer to its problems and to fulfill the tasks which it constantly sets for each individual."[3] I hope that you will find some of the answers you need in this book and that you will move in the direction you want to go.

References

1. Marion, P. Crisis Proof Your Career. New York, N.Y.: Berkley Books, 1994, p. 128.

2. Ibid. p. 129.

3. Frankl, V. Man's Search for Meaning. New York, N.Y.: Washington Square Press, 1985, p.98.

Contents

Chapter One

What Jobs Will Be There in the Future?

Physicians often ask me what kinds of jobs there will be for physician executives in the future. I have interviewed two futurists and four recruiters to get their opinions about what they are doing now and what they will be doing.

The Futurists

Mike Annison, July 5, 2005—futurist

Mike Annison, an often-quoted futurist, describes seven areas in which physician executives will be needed in the health care systems of tomorrow. Prior to forming his present consulting group, he was Vice President of the Naisbitt group whose research was the basis for the original best selling book *Megatrends*.

Restoring trust

The enormous challenge for physician executives in working with physicians, boards of trustees, and hospital administrators is to restore trust in the health care system.

There have been many abuses. One insurance company was raising rates for patients whose cost of care was beyond normal. So they classified everybody as abnormal and needing excessive care. The government sued them for hundreds of millions of dollars.

Doctors have ordered volumes of tests that may be unnecessary. In rare cases they have charged for drugs they have altered or watered down.

Trust needs to be restored among physicians, between hospitals and physicians, and between doctors and the general public:

- Among physicians—Doctors in different specialties are competing for the same work. For example endocarotid surgeries can be done by interventional radiologists; heart surgeons; or, in a couple of cases, even general surgeons. Physician executives will be wrestling with how to determine who has privileges for which procedure.

- Between hospitals and physicians—Physician executives will deal with how to manage the competition between hospitals and doctors for diagnostic services, ambulatory care services, and outpatient surgery.

- Between doctors and the general public on clinical mistakes—There is an article in the *Journal of American Medical Association* that says physicians are the third leading cause of death in the United States; 225,000 people each year die—12,000 because of unnecessary surgery, 7,000 because of medical errors, 20,000 because of other errors in hospitals, 80,000 because of infections, 106,000 because of the negative impacts of drugs.

2. Improving quality of care

Physician executives will have a central role in working with hospitals, doctors, private payers, and others on the quality of care and what it means. The issues are improving care, reducing costs, and making systems safer.

In the early 1900s, Ernest Codnam, a physician at Harvard medical school who practiced at Massachusetts General Hospital, was thrown off the staff for suggesting that doctors publish the results of the quality of care they provided.

Today, as a result of the work of CMS, the Quality Forum, Leap Frog group, and others, hospitals are reporting data to their boards of trustees. Every month hospital executives stand up and tell hospital trustees the state of quality on things such as fall rates, infections, and returns to surgery. This started to be done about 5 years ago and now is routine in most well-run hospitals.

3. Simplification

Health care is a complex system that it is very hard to understand, very hard to manage, and very expensive. If you can simplify processes and eliminate the number of times people do things differently, the quality goes up. Only about 30 percent of medicine in the United States today is evidence-based, in which a doctor follows a protocol based on scientific understanding of how to treat the disease. The rest is based on the doctor's understanding or how they were trained or any one of a number of other variables.

In an operating room if you standardize equipment and surgical instruments and simplify a host of activities, you improve care. If all the charts are available at seven in the morning before the doctor makes rounds, patients get better care and can be discharged earlier.

4. Technology

Physician executives are going to get stretched on dealing with technology. All technologies get smaller, faster, and cheaper, which means they move from major research centers to community hospitals and then to smaller rural hospitals. X-rays used to be sophisticated technology in hospitals. Then they moved to smaller hospitals and then into doctors' offices.

When clinical technologies move to a new location for clinical reasons, the process usually works well with no problems. When they move because of financial reasons, there are all kinds of conflicts and battles. The physician executive will be managing this process.

You can now visit a couple of places and watch doctors with hand-held PDAs pull up patients' record right in front of them. Patients feel good about it because they think their doctors know what is going on.

There is an explosion of small technologies. Using a computer a physician will guide a machine that is one molecule in size into a human body through a port, and it will simply extract cancer cells and bring them out.

Entire businesses are doing remote radiology. The physician can simply transmit data over communication systems, do the analysis in Timbuktu and then transmit the results back to where the care is being provided. Diagnostics are substituting for other procedures. Interventional radiologists rather than surgeons are doing the intervention, and the services are going to geographically remote places. Many new drugs in the areas of cardiology will enable us to avoid invasive surgery altogether.

Jeff Goldsmith, a futurist from Charlottesville, VA, says, "In the intensive care world you've seen emergence of remote practice models and sort of telemedicine 6.0. There is a company in Maryland that has been very successful in extending the reach of trained intensivists. The physician can look at the patient on a monitor, talk to them on the phone or talk to the intensive care nurse who is actually touching the patient. It dramatically increases the productivity of clinicians and enables them to manage patients in 4 or 5 locations, not just one physical location."

5. Privileges

Physician executives are going to manage the transition from credentialing people according to their specialty—you can do this because you are a heart surgeon—to credentialing people because of their capability—you can do this because you have shown me you can do it. Those battles are part of every single medical staff in the United States today.

The traditional function of the hospital medical staff was to ensure the quality of medicine within the hospital, but now there are all kinds of physicians who don't go near the hospital because hospitalists take care of their patients when they are admitted. The physician executive will be managing the relationships and standards for these two groups. The standards in a hospital will deal with more serious and sophisticated cases and be quite different from what is done on a routine one-hour surgical procedure down the street at the local surgical center.

Now they are working out the tasks of the hospitalists and how they will relate to multispecialty groups, primary care groups, outlying physicians or others.

6. Science of Medicine

Physician executives will manage the debate between traditional and non-traditional, complementary medicine. The state and federal legislatures are expanding the services that are eligible for payment under public programs. So far the debate has been about turf and boundaries, but the underlying issue has to do with role of science in medicine.

Medicine has always been an art and a science. A scientific approach is based on three attributes. First, the phenomenon is observable, you can see it. I do heart surgery, you walk. Second, it is quantifiable—53 people died, 47 lived. Third, it is repeatable. If I do this to Mary and it works, I know I can do it to Susie, Johnny, and Willie and it will work.

There is a lot in the art of medicine that doesn't show up that way. A physician told of caring for a patient he had known for 20 years—a 55 year old white male. When they completed his annual physical, the doctor had his hand on the door knob and said, "Is there anything else we ought to talk about?" The patient said, "Not really. The only thing I guess I might have mentioned is that I am a little winded going up stairs." The doctor turned around and said, "Tell me about it." It was the first symptom of an impending heart attack. That is the art of medicine—the doctor understood the importance of what seemed insignificant to the patient.

Navigating the science and the debates within the field about traditional medicine and others is going to stir up all kinds of trouble. The hardest part is that the only difference between an herb and a drug is FDA approval. Physician executives will be in middle of all the debates.

7. Finance

Physician executives will be dealing with who pays and how. Maintaining physician income is difficult in light of continuing pressure from the federal government, state governments, and third-party payers to lower reimbursement. I keep trying to get physicians to learn how to simplify and manage their business essentials sensibly. They need to work with hospitals so they don't waste time-probably 20 percent of their time is wasted because hospitals and physicians won't do things efficiently and effectively.

Mike Annison described the hot issues physician executives will be overseeing.

Jeff Goldsmith, July 2005—futurist

Jeff Goldsmith made predictions about who will be practicing and where. He says 38 percent of physicians are over 50. If we see a sustained recovery in the stock market, a large chunk of them will transition into other work. I don't think all of those folks will leave the health system—a lot of them will become medical directors, group practice CEOs, and heads of health systems and health plans.

The '90s were a period of frantic experimentation with new forms of organizing physicians. A lot of those experiments failed. We are going to see new forms of physician organizations in the next 10 years—many will be for profit and take advantage of what we have already seen in radiology, which is the ability of physicians to use broadband Internet connection to practice from anywhere.

The reach of one physician can be expanded using technology. When you are analyzing data including digital files as opposed to actually touching patients, it is going to change the way in which physicians practice.

Jeff Goldsmith says, "In the intensive care world, you've seen the emergence of remote practice models and sort of telemedicine 6.0. There is a company in Maryland that has been very successful in extending the reach of trained intensivists. Physicians can look at patients on a monitor, talk to them on the phone, or talk to intensive care nurses who are actually touching patients. The technology dramatically increases the productivity of clinicians and enables them to manage patients in 4 or 5 locations not just one physical location."

The Recruiters

Jennifer Grebenschikoff, Physician Executive Management Center, June 30, 2005

The chief medical officer type jobs are still important. I am using that as a generic title to cover all sorts of positions in which a physician executive is in a senior leadership role in the organization. The emphasis is clearly on patient safety and quality of care. We are seeing lots of different titles—VP of Medical Management, Chief Quality Officer, Executive VP for Medical Management.

The chief medical officer (CMO) role is going to become more and more comprehensive. It is so different today than what it was 5 years ago. It will be different again 5 years from now, but right now the big emphasis is on quality of care and outcomes.

Quality and Outcomes

Physician executives are helping organizations develop or change their cultures to embrace the whole idea that quality of care—clinical outcomes, patient satisfaction, and patient safety—are what they are all about. Payers are paying for it; consumers are demanding it; and malpractice insurers are saying—if you can't show me that you are providing really good patient care, we are not going to cover you or we are going to make it prohibitively expensive for you to practice.

When I go to an organization that says it wants to be the safest hospital with the highest quality outcomes, it wants a physician executive who will help it be accountable for what it has promised to do. There are pathways or guidelines in use so that every patient who has a particular diagnosis gets a consistent pattern of care.

Examples: We have set a goal that 80 percent of patients arriving in the ER who we think have pneumonia will get antibiotics within 4 hours or less. Our goal is to have 90 percent of all patients presenting with heart attack symptoms get beta blockers within 24 hours of arrival.

They come up with a chart called a score card to measure it monthly or quarterly. I ask to see them. I want to see that there are more green blocks than yellow and red blocks on the score card. Once they have mostly green blocks, they raise the target.

The CMO does the literature search and says, "Your American College of Cardiology says that these things work. Here is how we are going to be measured. If we don't do these things we're not going to be able to meet the goal that insurers, payers, and employers in the community have set for us."

The credentialing and privileging committees are now starting to use compliance with metrics as a reappointment issue: "If you don't do this, we will be discussing it at your reappointment." I don't personally know of a hospital that has said we won't give you privileges because you have consistently refused to use pathways. They tend to say, "How can we help you use these pathways?"

The same logic applies when they start to put in electronic medical records or computerized order entry. There are doctors who just don't type, and they don't want to. They work around it with voice recognition dictation. Or they ask, "Do you want us to send you to typing school? Do you want us to give you computer lessons? What do you need to make you effective in this system that everyone else is going to be using?"

Who Is Getting Those Jobs?

When I do a search, I do not consider physicians who haven't become involved in management yet. They have moved up internally to become associate or assistant medical directors. Sometimes they already have the title of CMO and are moving to a larger system or in some cases making a lateral move.

Any potential CMO needs to develop a list that shows how their organization is better as a result of their leadership. Not that they saw so many patients or that they brought in so many cases for surgery. How have they reduced length of stay, been the chair for the committee that works on the clinical care guidelines for pneumonia, been involved in the 100,000 lives campaign that IHI is doing, evaluated and made recommendations about which clinical information technology to buy, been a champion who encouraged others to come along, They need to show that they have influenced people by how they say things and what they say.

What Do They Do in the Jobs?

There are not a lot of reasons these days for primary care physicians to spend time at hospitals. Hospitalists are caring for their patients. The medical staff by-laws say everyone on the staff has responsibility for ER call. The doctors are saying, "Why should I take call? I don't admit my patients there anymore."

A lot of organizations don't have quarterly medical staff meetings anymore. They have them once a year. It is too expensive for physicians to take time away from their practices. When they are seeing Medicare or Medicaid patients and getting four dollars for every ten that they bill, they don't want to sit on a committee whose members are doing nothing but talk.

Hospitals and health systems want to find ways to relate to primary care physicians in a way that has some value to the physicians as well as to the hospital. No one quite has an answer to that, but my clients say bring me a CMO who has figured out how to do this.

Credentialing and Privileging Issues

With increased competition and the increased need for physicians to find revenue-producing activity comes a lot of turf and territory issues. The big one right now is—who gets to do carotid stents? Is it the vascular surgeon, the cardiologist, the radiologist, or all three? Some say, "We will allow everyone to do it, but they have to do so many procedures a year." Others say, "After such and such a date, we are going to cut off two specialties and only the third specialty gets to do these."

Research, Analyze, Present, Persuade

CMOs need to find the information, distill it, analyze it, summarize it, condense it, and present it and then be the politician, mediator, and negotiator to try to help people come to a decision that is right for patients. The value of CMOs is that their focus is always on how this is going to make patient care better. It's not about the hospital, the doctors, or the nurses—it's about the patient. When I interview candidates and they start talking to me about how they improve the quality of care to patients, I know I've got a real CMO. There are some CMOs who understand that they are joined at hip with the Chief Nursing Executive. Those are candidates I can present.

Clinical Information

The clinical information area is rolling along so quickly—electronic medical records, Web portals, paperless organizations, wireless organizations, computerized physician order entry, all of the activity that allows them to be effective in the way they gather information about a patient and share that information and how quickly it can be done. Candidates who don't have that interest or expertise are going to be lost.

They don't have to know how to install a computer system, but they do have to be the champions, to say to the medical staff, "This is a good thing and here's why. Here's how it will be positive for all of us."

It is not going away no matter what we read about two or three hospitals here and there having disasters in their systems. They'll come back and get it right the second time. Everyone is learning from all those errors, so in the future there will be fewer and fewer errors.

Only the big systems have chief medical information officers (CMIOs). There are not many of them because that is another physician executive you have to pay. Sometimes they are part time, even in a larger system. Systems with ten or more hospitals might have a part-time CMIO who is still doing something else in a practice. As systems get larger and larger, you see full-time CMIO.

Physician Leadership Development

Every physician executive should be measured on how well he or she puts in place a physician leadership development program. They should look at the medical staff, decide whom they will nominate to serve as chair of a committee or as the secretary/ treasurer of the medical staff in five years.

You can look at someone's background and see that a person was always meant to be a leader. He or she was the chief resident, president of the medical school class, the Eagle Scout in high school. The person had leadership ability and their peers recognized that. Such physicians are always out there, but they need to be supported, nurtured, educated. Say to them, "We understand that your time is valuable. Here's how we want to help you develop that leadership capacity. You don't have to become a physician executive per se, but we would like to have your leadership ability somewhere on this medical staff organization." That means sending them to leadership programs or bringing programs in, mentoring them one on one. It means spending a little money, but it's an investment, not an expense.

Presentations

Communities want to know what the doctor says on clinical issues. The executives or CMOs (or whatever physician executive title they are using) are usually the ones who represent the hospital. They need to be able to make presentations in the community, in the region, at the state legislature, and to the Joint Commission on Accreditation of Healthcare Organizations and other regulatory agencies. They need to get their points across on TV and radio, to community groups, and elsewhere.

Carol Westfall, Cejka Search, July 7, 2005

Want Kinds of Jobs Are Out There for Physician Executives?

The traditional titles of positions we are placing in hospitals, health systems, and managed care organization are CMO, VPMA, medical director, associate medical director, director or associate director of clinical research, chief quality officer, and chief and chair of departments. Some new titles are chief clinical officer or senior VP of research and development.

Health care CEOs are recognizing they can't go it alone. They need more physician leaders. We did a survey that showed CEOs in the top 100 hospitals in the country all had CMOs. Those in the middle were showing an increasing rate of hiring CMOs.

Physician executives can look at how to manage care of people from prevention to home care to hospice. They use their clinical and business skills to evaluate technologies, services, and programs and say, "Here is what we need to do to get some good outcomes." They are answering these questions: What do we need now? What are we going to need 5 years from now? How should we be spending our money? Who are the top orthopedists in town? Where are the best outcomes for cardiovascular services achieved? We think this is driven by pay for performance as reimbursement between the hospital and the physician becomes intertwined.

If an appendectomy in New York City costs three times as much as it does in St. Louis, Missouri, something is happening in St. Louis to be able to do things cheaper. It's not just because things cost more in New York. It could be the length of stay after surgery is 3 days in New York and 2 days in St Louis. Physician executives are researching the best practices and getting them accepted in their organizations.

We are also placing heads of specialty centers—heart, cancer, women's health, neuroscience institutes. The titles are VP, Director, Administrator, or CEO. Sometimes the centers are separate from the hospital, sometimes a joint partnership with the hospital, sometimes owned by physicians. They are more often hospital or system driven because it is so expensive to get them going. They will take either a physician or a non-physician for the head role. A physician in that position is more expensive and can be threatening to a non-physician CEO, but some see that it is going to be worth the money.

Some people are getting pharmaceutical jobs, but they are usually on an inside track and invited to apply for the position. They are in private practice doing clinical trials or being paid to speak at conferences. I talked to a guy in one of those jobs and he loves it. Because he has good public speaking skills, he was doing sales presentations for them. He has been there four years and is getting some international experience. They want him to assess business opportunities—should they buy another company or get into a different area. He has other cardiologists reporting to him so he is getting management experience, but it is primarily about overseeing the clinical trials and making sure that they are clinically sound.

Managed care companies are pretty healthy now compared to a couple of years ago. They had built up their medical teams and then they downsized. There is more consolidation. They don't have as many positions to apply for, but most health plans offered in the work place have a managed care option. It is one of several choices, and if it has good outcomes, people might choose it because it is less expensive.

Who Is Getting the Positions?

For CMO, VPMA, and medical director jobs, clients want someone who has done that job in a comparable size system or in a slightly smaller system so the job would be a step up. You wouldn't come into that job directly from a clinical role unless you were a known entity and were being promoted from within the organization. With the competition as it is right now, you have to obtain one of these positions in your own organization before you can go somewhere else and do it. A 300-bed hospital wants a VPMA with VPMA experience.

It used to be if you led committees and became president of the medical staff, you could become an associate medical director somewhere, but the competition is stiffer now. Leading committees won't be enough. It is going to be how you market yourself.

I talked to a physician yesterday who has not had his first full-time position yet, but he is sharp. I could tell it on the phone. He called the hospital, got to the secretary of the board member who is in charge of the search, got the cell phone of the board member, called the board member, had a conversation in a very appropriate way and told him, "I am not qualified for your CEO job, but I'm a Senior VP, and I want you to know about me." That's big. He will make it. Doctors don't usually do that.

Even though the competition is stiff, there is always room for stellar candidates who look good, sound good, have good manners, present well, and can quantify and articulate their results.

Some Marketing Tips

- *Create an interesting and enticing career "story."* Keep it concise and consistent. Memorize it. "Here's what I've done; here's what I want to do; here's what I can do for your organization."

- *Quantify your results.* Clearly describe and articulate your results and accomplishments, using numbers whenever possible in your resume and when being interviewed.

- *Develop name recognition and demonstrate your competence.* Speak. Write articles. Volunteer your skills.

- *Build relationships.* Don't wait to be called; don't wait for the "right" job. Continuously build relationships with people you know and people you don't know. Call key decision-makers and let them know who you are and what you can do for them, even if they don't currently have a job opening or you're not qualified for the job opening they *do* have.

- *Be persistent.* If your call is not taken right away, try again. If you can't get through to the CEO, talk with the COO, or the Board Chair, or the CEO's secretary! Keep your name in front of them.

Qualities to emphasize throughout all conversations, interactions, and paperwork:

- High-energy
- Results-driven
- Strategic yet hands-on
- Integrity
- Decisiveness
- Change agent
- Risk-taker
- Common sense and street smarts
- Respected

Susan Cejka, Grant Cooper Associates, June 20, 2005

The competition for physician executive positions is fierce. We just did a search for an entry-level medical director. The candidate that we placed had been managing 27 medical directors. He was fabulous. He was a senior medical director from an organization in the same city who took a step back to become a regular medical director because he didn't want to relocate. He brought competitive information with him. The candidate got his organization to give him a written release to get out of the non-compete clause. He was very well thought of in the organization, but his position had been cut because of an acquisition. He took a huge salary cut and job cut to stay in the field.

Now you say–how am I going to break into the field when we are seeing this type of result? Managed care was always the way to break in. You were tainted if you tried to move from managed care to a hospital, but it still could happen. It's tougher now.

I think the field of VPMA in hospitals is still alive and well. However, if there is a search firm involved,we are always going to be recruiting an experienced person from another hospital. For that position we will never be recruiting someone without experience. To get your feet in, you still come up the normal way where you chair committees, become chief of staff, then you sneak into getting a part-time paid position, but that sneaking in has to be done in your own organization.

Let's do three buckets—managed care, hospitals and group practices, and academics.

Managed care is not a great field for medical directors right now because the prevailing theory in all managed care companies is we are not going to do preauthorizations or second opinions. So we don't need as many medical directors. There is no such thing as managed care any more; there is just an insurance company that is paying some bills. Choice won. The American public is angry about its health care bills, but it got choice, and that is what it wanted.

The field of hospitals and group practice is stable. The same number of positions exists. The field is not expanding because we are not adding new hospitals and new big group practices. You have to be a hospital of certain size and sophistication to have a medical director—300 beds. I get blind sided sometimes and find a 600-bed hospital that doesn't have one, but in general the magic number is 300. You always need new ones because you have people retiring.

I think academics is a booming field because tenure doesn't mean anything any more. They have separated tenure from money. They can't fire you, but they don't have to pay you. They get less and less money because of no raises and less reimbursement from the government.

I hardly place any group practice medical directors anymore because there are so few left, but I am doing a lot of department chair searches. Those are really good jobs with lots of responsibilities.

I am in the process of doing seven department chairs for the Methodist hospital in Houston, a 900-bed teaching hospital. If you are in a medical school, the next logical step up is a dean so it gets pretty skinny there, but if you are department chair in a large community hospital, your next logical move is VPMA.

One organization paid an orthopedist chair $800,000 and gave him a $6 million budget to rebuild the department. The department was a disaster. Most of the doctors didn't speak to each other. They would pass notes. People wouldn't show up for call. They would get invited to go on a medical device junket and would go away for 2 weeks with 3 days notice. They had lots of screamers and throwers. There were 21 people in the department. He had to fire all but 7 of them and recruit new people. The hospital had been in the midst of a big turn around, and they just had not gotten around to dealing with the problems.

What Else Do You See on the Horizon?

It has been a long time since managed care died, and there hasn't been a next new thing. We are really due for a next new thing. There are two that seem to be bubbling up—one is consumer-directed health care and the other is pay for performance.

Consumer-directed health care shifts the burden of payment to the public. Everyone will have catastrophic insurance, but, for the rest, we make the decisions about how we are going to spend our health care money. My deductible is $1000, and that's going to get worse, but we do have choice, don't we?

We are going to have physician profiles and hospital profiles, and they are going to show the quality of their outcomes and their cost. The information will be published and the managed care organization is going to pay the doctor and the hospital differently based on their quality outcomes and their costs. HMOs want to pay you less if you are really expensive and more if you're not as expensive

Lee Newcomer started a company that was pay for performance, and he got stonewalled by all the hospitals in the country and the company couldn't make a go of it. He folded it back into United Health, the theory being that United has the clout to pull it off. However, in St. Louis all the hospitals have refused to sign the United contract because it has pay for performance in it.

Larry Tyler, Tyler and Company, July 2005

Tyler and Company does many types of searches—CEOs, VPMAs, CMOs, academic department chairs, and service line medical directors for oncology, women's health, etc.

We are still placing people in VPMA jobs, but there is not fast growth. Most of the hospitals that are going to have VPMAs already have them. At one point there was a fast ramp up—everyone was trying to put in a new VPMA—but now it is mostly vacancies occurring because of retirements or because somebody left.

When someone comes to us and is willing to pay our fee, they are looking for someone who meets their specifications—someone who was in a VPMA slot somewhere else. Right now the supply of good candidates that have already been VPMAs is pretty good.

If you lead committees and become president of the medical staff, you can become a VPMA in your own place. To do that, you have to have a lot going for you, which means you have a great personality. You probably have to have a sponsor on the medical staff—someone who has worked with you and knows you well.

If you become an associate VPMA job in your own place, you could parlay that into a

VPMA position somewhere else. You wouldn't go from being the President of the Medical Staff at Piedmont Hospital to being a VPMA as Moses Cone Hospital. It just wouldn't happen unless you had gone to medical school with a third of the docs on the search committee. It's too wide a gap for a stranger to cover.

We will continue to have VPMAs in hospitals. There is much pressure to not add positions to a hospital, but hospital systems that have eliminated the hospital VPMA and kept the regional or corporate VPMA are going to regret that decision. I think they will be forced to have doctors at each hospital.

I am disappointed that VPMAs are not seeking operating experience so they can become CEOs. They are sticking with things that are in their comfort zone—medical staff relations, quality. I don't see enough of them saying, "Give me the dietary department, give me housekeeping, give me the entire ER operation."

Physicians could head not just the clinical but also the operational part of a cancer center or a cardiology program. If they become vice president for cardiology services, they would have the dual role of being both clinician and administrator.

VPMAs think they want to be in the top position because they see a guy sitting in an office making decisions and they think, "I can do that." What they don't realize is that the decisions are based on something besides education. They are based upon experience. A non-physician CEO can approach a problem saying I've been there and done that. A physician can't necessarily do that.

I think the failure of physician executives to become CEOs is based on a lack of interest and an unwillingness to take the risks. Some of them want to be CEOs, but they want to wait around until the CEO retires and be promoted from the VPMA position. That happens occasionally, but they would be viable candidates somewhere else if they had operations experience.

If they are not going get operations experience, I'd bone up on the quality stuff. The whole quality movement not only still has steam but seems to be picking up steam. Report cards are measuring outcomes. CMS just put out one that people are not jumping to but the fact that they have it there means they will keep working on it, and it will become more important. This is also driven by the safety measure.

Everyone I interviewed said competition is fierce in the market right now. The best path is to move up into a management position in your own organization, and then you can go somewhere else for the next one. Candidates who can produce results, who speak and write well, who can be pleasant while also being directive when needed, who get out of their offices and talk to people, and who can persuade physicians to change behavior will be desirable to hiring organizations.

Chapter Two

Life-Work Planning
Can Give You Energy

Now that you've read about the types of jobs that people in the know predict will exist in the future, I'd like you to back away from the specifics of the profession and take a careful look at your own career thus far. What are the characteristics of your work experience and your personal life? The assessment of these areas is the first step in a process commonly referred to as Life-Work Planning.

The term implies that you can plan your life and your work and not just let events happen to you. You plan and then relax—not holding onto the plan too tightly. Most things I've wanted desperately have come to me after I let up from desperately wanting them. I turned my attention to something else, and then what I desired seemed to just come and sit in my lap. But this does not mean that you passively wait. You set goals, write them down, and then do activities that work toward the goals and that can make you enjoy life's journey.

In order to plan your future, it is a good idea to take time to assess your career—think about the present, take a look back at your past, and then look toward the future with a plan of action. I am going to discuss ways to examine your present with the help of some writing exercises and an overview of an instrument that measures your likes and dislikes. Writing is an excellent way to examine your life. It can enable you to do life-work planning on your own.

Begin by making a list of energizers and deenergizers. Use the work sheets at the end of the chapter. (Such work sheets will appear in most of the chapters so that you can become involved with the techniques prescribed in this book immediately.) Energizers are activities or people that excite you. You have more energy after doing them or being with them than you did when you began. Deenergizers are activities or people who drain you of energy quickly. You feel tired and maybe even depressed after a short time.

Examples of Energizers

My List

- Speaking to a large group

- One-on-one educational coaching sessions

- Half-hour walk at the end of the day
- Talk with a good friend
- Art projects
- Dancing
- Writing

A Physician's List

- Helping colleagues or patients solve problems
- Completing tasks in a timely manner
- Talking with a good friend
- Serious exercise or competitive sports

Examples of Deenergizers

My List

- Continuous conflict
- Trying to work when there is a lot of noise
- Filing papers
- Parties with large numbers of people (unless there is dancing)
- Preparing income tax records

A Physician's List

- Long and/or disorganized meetings
- Confronting a fellow physician about something unpleasant
- Budget preparation

After you've made these lists, I suggest filling out a personality instrument called the Myers-Briggs Type Indicator to help you further understand why you like some activities and don't like others. It reinforces for you why some things turn you on and others turn you off.

To find out who gives the test in your area, contact the headquarters of the Association for Psychological Type, 816/444-3500, and ask it for an APT chapter in your area. We give the test in ACPE's Career Advancement services and in educational programs that can be brought to your organization—contact Barbara Linney at blinney@acpe.org.

It's important to know what your natural tendencies are when you are making career changes. I have heard physicians say that they are living a life that a 10-year-old boy or girl chose for them. Many were that young when they made the decision to become doctors. One obstetrician told me he wished he had filled out the instrument in high school. He would never have chosen his specialty, obstetrics/gynecology, if he had known how much time alone he needed and how much interruptions bothered him.

The Myers-Briggs Type Indicator is based on Carl Jung's works. Jung, a Swiss psychiatrist (1875-1961) "believed we are born with a predisposition to certain personality prefer-ences."[1] He came up with four sets of behaviors to describe how people usually behave. Katherine Briggs had been devising her own classification of personality differences when she read Jung and realized their theories were similar, but his were more thoroughly devel-oped. "In 1942, prompted by World War I...and the conviction that the war was caused, in part, by people not understanding differences," Katherine Briggs and her daughter, Isabel Myers, "began to develop a series of questions to measure personality differences. The result was the Myers-Briggs Type Indicator."[2]

I'm going to briefly describe the behaviors in hopes that you will be able to say, "Yes, I'm somewhat like that one but not like that one," and then perhaps you will want to pursue the information further. The four sets of behaviors are:

> Extrovert.............................Introvert
> Sensing...............................Intuitive
> Thinking.............................Feeling
> Judging ....Perceiving

The sets of behaviors describe our source of energy, how we take in information from the world, how we make decisions, and how we organize our lives. As you are deciding which behavior you prefer, keep in mind that everyone exhibits all eight behaviors, but most peo-ple have at least a slight preference and often a strong preference for one behavior in each of the sets. Just as people can use both their hands for many actions, they usually have a pref-erence for one when it comes to writing, throwing, hammering, cutting, etc.

The first set (Extrovert and Introvert) explains our source of energy. (Try to forget society's definition of these two words—outgoing and shy. Jung used them differently.) Extroverts get energy from people and from activities outside themselves. They want to talk to others a lot, often working out their thoughts aloud as they talk. Introverts get energy from within them-selves. They usually need a fair amount of time alone and prefer to do their thinking quiet-ly to themselves and then let others know what they have worked out.

Extroverts begin to talk and then, seven or eight sentences later, they know what they real-ly think. Introverts often think extroverts have lied to them at the beginning of the con-versation, but it's not necessarily so. They are just working through a problem out loud while the Introvert would do all the thinking internally and then deliver the finished product.

Similarly, Extroverts can be annoyed with Introverts because they resent that Introverts didn't let them in on any of their quiet thinking process.

"If you don't know what an Extrovert is thinking...you haven't been listening, because he or she will tell you. If you don't know what an Introvert is thinking...you haven't asked, or, in some cases, you haven't waited long enough for an answer....Introverts 'bake' their ideas inside, much as cake is cooked in the oven and presented to the outside world only after it is finished."[3]

Kroeger and Thuesen write, "If you are an Extrovert, you tend to talk first, think later, and don't know what you'll say until you hear yourself say it....You probably know a lot of people and count many of them among your 'close friends'....If you are an Introvert, you probably rehearse things before saying them and prefer that others would do the same....You like to share special occasions with just one other person or perhaps a few close friends."[4]

At work, Extroverts like variety and action. They like to have lots of people around in the working environment. Introverts at work like quiet for concentration, and they can work alone contentedly for long periods.

"An Extraverted employee was frustrated because his Introverted colleague withdrew and became uncommunicative when he tried to confront some work-related issues. The Introverted colleague defended her withdrawal by commenting that she was unable to offer her viewpoints because the frustrated co-worker was aggressive and overbearing. Both learned to accommodate the other's communication style. The Extravert learned to state issues calmly and set a time in the future to discuss issues. This gave the Introvert time to think about and prepare for a discussion. The Introvert learned to express her opinions more openly. The Extravert slowed the pace of the conversation so that his co-worker could process the information and formulate a response."[5]

Physician executives who are Extroverts probably enjoy most the part of the job that requires that they speak to groups or walk around the medical facility talking with co-workers. Introverts may be most comfortable managing information or doing quality assurance and utilization review.

"...the American population is about equally divided between Extraverts and Introverts....If you are having trouble deciding which you prefer, ask yourself this question: 'If I had to be one way or the other for the rest of my life, which would I choose?'"[6]

Before you read about the next set of behaviors, write the answers to the following questions on the work sheets at the end of the chapter:

- Which term seems to describe how you like to do things, Extrovert or Introvert? Give one reason why.

- Is your life structured so you can do enough of this behavior to satisfy you? If so, how? If not, what could you change? Example for Extrovert—I keep my office door open so people can drop in any time. Example for Introvert—I stay at work an hour after every one leaves so I can collect my thoughts and prepare for the next day.

The second set of behaviors (Sensing and Intuitive) describe how we take in information about our world. Sensing types take in information through their five senses (sight, sound, smell, taste, and touch). Intuitives take in information through almost a sixth sense or a hunch. They think they know something, are not sure why, but are right often enough that they come to trust their hunches.

Sensing types like to work with details, and they approach projects in a step-by-step manner, starting at the beginning and proceeding until they are finished. They like established ways of doing things. These people often like to be involved with finance or technology and are very comfortable with numbers, computers, detailed procedures, etc. Because they don't mind repetition, their motto might be, "If it isn't broken, don't fix it."

Whereas Sensing types are very comfortable with proven methods, Intuitives rarely like to do the same thing twice. Their motto might be the same as the title of the management book: *If It Ain't Broken, Break It.*[7] They like to start big projects, sometimes tackling the middle section first and skipping around from one idea to the next without a particular order. Intuitives see the big picture. They are often looking toward the future and imagining possibilities.

Intuitives often like executive positions where they are responsible for strategic planning or are called upon to solve unexpected problems. They often serve in counselor roles no matter what titles they have because they enjoy helping people think of possible changes they might make in their lives.

Thinking about patients that you have dealt with can help you know which you prefer. "Patients with a preference for Sensing are interested in factual details of their condition, prefer step-by-step explanations, and ask practical questions. Those with a preference for Intuition are more likely to ask long-term speculative questions, seek new solutions (for examples, alternative or complementary medicine), want multiple options."[8]

If you show a peanut to Sensing types, they see a small brown object that is rough and appears to be two ball shapes joined together. Show it to Intuitives and their first response might be, "Reese's peanut butter cups. George Washington Carver did experiments on peanuts." They will think of something beyond what they are actually looking at. These two types often annoy each other because of their different styles, but if they can work together without driving each other crazy, good things happen. Intuitives start some great projects and Sensing types help them finish them, tending to many of the details. Each needs the other.

"If you are a Sensor, you probably prefer specific answers to questions; when you ask someone the time, you prefer 'three fifty-two' and get irritated if the answer is 'a little before four' or almost time to go....If you are an Intuitive, you probably would rather fantasize about spending your next paycheck than sit and balance your checkbook."[9]

Sensors focus on "what is," while Intuitives focus on "what could be." "About 65 percent of the American population are Sensors."[10]

Before you read about the next set of behaviors, write the answers to the following questions on the work sheets:

- Which term seems to describe how you like to do things, Sensing or Intuitive? Give one reason why.

- Is your life structured so you can do enough of this behavior to satisfy you? If so, how? If not, what could you change? Example for Sensing—I enjoy reading through the financial statement to see if it is correct in every way. Example for Intuitive—I look at the bottom line of the financial statement first. If it is what it should be, I glance at the rest. If not, I look for where the problems are.

Once you've taken in information from your world, it's usually necessary to make decisions about it. The two sets of behaviors (Thinking and Feeling) explain how people prefer to make decisions. Thinking types make decisions based on what is logical and reasonable. Feeling types consider how the decision will affect other people and themselves.

Thinking types are very good at analyzing business plans or problems. They are often firm and tough-minded and may hurt other people's feelings without knowing it. If it makes economical sense to fire someone, they can do it without agonizing over the decision.

Whereas Thinking types decide with their heads, Feeling types decide with their hearts. Feeling types can and do fire people when necessary, but they suffer when they have to do it because they worry about hurting people's feelings and about the hardship such actions will cause employees' families. Feeling types are good at understanding people. They like harmony and are willing to work to make it happen. "When Thinkers and Feelers clash, more often than not the Feeler ends up hurt and angry, while the Thinker is confused about what went wrong."[11]

"If you are a Thinker, you probably think it's more important to be right than liked; you don't believe it is necessary to like people in order to be able to work with them and do a good job....If you are a Feeler, you probably put yourself in other people's moccasins; you are likely to be the one in a meeting who asks, 'How will this affect the people involved?'"[12]

It's important to remember that Thinking types have deep feelings and that Feeling types think logically. Jung and the Myers-Briggs Type Indicator refer to how people make decisions, not to their ability to think or feel.

"The American population is evenly split between Thinkers and Feelers. However, this is the only type dimension in which clear gender differences show up. About two thirds of men prefer thinking, and about two thirds of women prefer feeling."[13]

Before you read about the next set of behaviors, write the answers to the following questions on your work sheets:

- Which term seems to describe how you like to do things, Thinking or Feeling? Give one reason why.

- Is your life structured so you can do enough of this behavior to satisfy you? If so, how? If not, what could you change?

The final sets of behaviors (Judging and Perceiving) describe how you organize your life. Judging types like to make decisions and get things settled quickly. They like to have order and structure, giving them a sense that they have life under control. Perceiving types like to continue to take in more information and keep their options open. They like to take each experience as it comes, without the feeling of being tied down to a plan.

"If you are a Judger, you probably thrive on order; you have a special system for keeping things in the refrigerator and dish drainer, hangers in your closets, and pictures on your walls....If you are a Perceiver, you don't believe that 'neatness counts,' even though you would prefer to have things in order; what's important is creativity, spontaneity, and responsiveness."[14]

Physician executives who are judging types are usually comfortable making decisions quickly—saying yes or no to a certain medical procedure on the basis of cost and quality of care. Perceiving types probably prefer tasks such as gathering a great deal of information before a piece of medical equipment is purchased.

"Judgers tend to live in an orderly way and are happiest when their lives are structured and matters are settled....Perceivers like to live in a spontaneous way and are happiest when their lives are flexible....Judgers seek to regulate and control life....Perceivers seek to understand life rather than control it."[15]

"The American population is evenly split on this dimension: 50 percent are Judgers, and 50 percent are Perceivers."[16]

Write the answers to the following questions in your workbooks:

- Which term seems to describe how you like to do things, Judging or Perceiving? Give one reason why.

- Is your life structured so you can do enough of this behavior to satisfy you? If so, how? If not, what could you change?

Remember—everyone can do all these different behaviors, but your comfort zone will tend to be in one area or the other of each of the pairs.

Once you understand your own preferences, you can make educated guesses about others in your work and personal life. Understanding another person's preferred style "reduces blame, criticism, defensiveness, and withholding, which are the major trip-ups in relationships."[17]

"The MBTI [Myers-Briggs Type Indicator] tool specifically aids team members by providing a neutral and affirmative language with which to discuss differences....and teaching team members to value and work with the strengths of others."[18]

If you can identify which type you are, you can more easily choose work that is satisfying to you. Also, if you decide which of these behaviors you prefer and structure your life so you get to do them, you will find you have more energy. Here is a list of activities that you can do that will meet the needs of your preferred type.

Extroverts—Plan activities to be with people.

Introverts—Plan to have time alone.

Sensing—Do something that lets you have control over details. Write computer programs. Have a detailed filing system. Plan an elaborate dinner.

Intuitive—Use your imagination to come up with new projects. Write them down. Try to carry out some of them.

Thinking—Write a financial plan. Run your own business.

Feeling—Get with a friend and talk about your feelings. Do something good for someone else. If you have been overdoing for other people, stop.

Judging—Be the one who makes decisions. You probably will not be happy unless you have the final say on some issues.

Perceiving—Gather information and let others make some of the decisions. Have an unscheduled Saturday when you do whatever occurs to you all day long.

Fill out the Myers-Briggs instrument some time to get a more accurate assessment. The information may help explain why some things energize you and others deenergize you.

Life-work planning may involve changing jobs, but it may not. If you decide what energizes you and what deenergizes you and accept that fact without condemning your inadequacies, you can add activities to your life that satisfy you. If you meet the needs of each of your behavior types, you'll have the energy not only to be productive in your present situation but to choose new challenges.

I have talked to many physicians who were somewhat disturbed that they wanted to do something besides clinical practice. Frankly, they were bored and wanted new challenges.

Their families and friends did not want to hear such comments and their general reaction was "You're a doctor. What more could you want?" The authors of *Do What You Are* explain this restlessness as a normal part of adult growth. "Based on our experience with our clients, we believe that mid-life marks the beginning of a new phase of type development. Unconsciously, we seek to round out our personalities and become more effective and capable....[H]aving reached the top of the proverbial hill, we may also reach some disturbing conclusions: first, that there may not be that much time left ahead, and, second, that there isn't much challenge in spending the remaining years exactly as we spent our earlier years."[19]

Bluestein conducted a survey of 230 physicians who changed from clinical practice to management. He interpreted the transition to an alternative career as a first cousin of mid-life crisis rather than a mid-career change. He said of his own change, "One of the primary motivations to do something else was looking down the road 30 years and realizing that most of my time was going to be spent doing pretty much the same old thing."[20]

Competition for physician executive positions is fierce. Health care organizations have merged, downsized, and gone out of business. Some experienced physician executives are taking entry level positions to stay in the field. However, recruiters say the people who are stars still get positions. If you have management experience, speak well, write well, play well with others, have financial savy, you can get a job.

The turnover of physician executives is high. My sources tell me that a physician executive now lasts about 2.7 years in one position. Whatever is causing you to think about making changes, try to stay calm and take the time to think about your life and work before you make decisions about what to do next.

References

1. Kroeger, O., and Thuesen, J. *Type Talk*. New York, N.Y.: Delacorte Press, 1988, p. 281.

2. Ibid., p. 282.

3. Tieger, P., and Barron-Tieger, B. *Do What You Are*. Boston, Mass.: Little, Brown, and Company, 2001, p. 15.

4. Kroeger, O., and Thuesen, J., *op. cit.*, pp. 14-15.

5. Dunning, Donna. *Introduction to Type and Communication*. Palo Alto, Calif.: CPP, Inc., 2003.

6. Tieger, P., and Barron-Tieger, B., *op. cit.*, p. 17.

7. Kriegel, R., and Patler, L. *If It Ain't Broke, Break It*. New York, N.Y.: Warner Books, 1991.

8. Kroeger, O., and Thuesen, J., *op. cit.*, pp. 18-19.

9. Allen, J., and Brock, S. *Health Care Communication Using Personality Type, Patients are Different*. London and Philadelphia: Routledge, Taylor & Francis Group, 2000.

10. Tieger, P., and Barron-Tieger, B., *op. cit.*, p. 21.

11. *Ibid.*, p. 23.

12. Kroeger, O., and Thuesen, J., *op. cit.*, p. 19.

13. Tieger, P., and Barron-Tieger, B., *op. cit.*, p. 24.

14. Kroeger, O., and Thuesen, J., *op. cit.*, p. 21.

15. Tieger, P., and Barron-Tieger, B., *op. cit.*, p. 25.

16. *Ibid.*, p. 29.

17. Laney, M. *The Introvert Advantage: How to Thrive in an Extrovert World.* New York, N.Y.: Workman Publishing, 2002, p. 97.)

18. Hirsh, E., Hirsh, K., and Hirsh, S. *Introduction to Type and Teams.* Palo Alto, Calif.: CPP, Inc., 2003.

19. Tieger, P., and Barron-Tieger, B., *op. cit.*, p. 87.

20. Bluestein, P. "Physicians in Transition." *Physician Executive* 21(12):16-24, Dec. 1995.

Other Readings

Keirsey, D., and Bates, M. *Please Understand Me.* Del Mar, Calif.: Prometheus Nemesis Book Company, 1984.

Myers, I., with Myers, P. *Gifts Differing.* Palo Alto, Calif.: Consulting Psychologists Press, Inc., 1980.

Work Sheets

At the end of many of the chapters in this book, we have provided space for you to undertake the exercises that have been recommended. We encourage you to take the time to fill them out. If, like my editor, you wince at the prospect of writing in a book, just make photocopies. The important thing is to record your thoughts on these important topics when the juices are running.

Energizers/Deenergizers

These are the things in my life that energize me:

1. _____
2. _____
3. _____
4. _____
5. _____
6. _____
7. _____
8. _____
9. _____
10. _____

These are the things in my life that deenergize me:

1. _____
2. _____
3. _____
4. _____
5. _____
6. _____
7. _____
8. _____
9. _____
10. _____

Behavior Sets

Extrovert/Introvert

1. Which term seems to describe how you like to do things, Extrovert or Introvert? Give one reason why.

_____

_____

_____

_____

_____

_____

2. Is your life structured so you can do enough of this behavior to satisfy you? If so, how? If not, what could you change?

_____

_____

_____

_____

_____

_____

Sensing/Intuitive

1. Which term seems to describe how you like to do things, Sensing or Intuitive? Give one reason why.

_____

_____

_____

_____

_____

_____

2. Is your life structured so you can do enough of this behavior to satisfy you? If so, how? If not, what could you change?

_____

_____

_____

_____

_____

_____

_____

Thinking/Feeling

1. Which term seems to describe how you like to do things, Thinking or Feeling? Give one reason why.

_____

_____

_____

_____

_____

_____

_____

2. Is your life structured so you can do enough of this behavior to satisfy you? If so, how? If not, what could you change?

_____

_____

_____

_____

_____

_____

Judging/Perceiving

1. Which term seems to describe how you like to do things, Judging or Perceiving? Give one reason why.

_____

_____

_____

_____

_____

_____

2. Is your life structured so you can do enough of this behavior to satisfy you? If so, how? If not, what could you change?

_____

_____

_____

_____

_____

_____

_____

Chapter Three

Know Where You've Been
Before You Decide Where to Go

In order to plan your future, it is a good idea to take time to think about the present, to take a look back at the past, and then to look toward the future with a plan of action. In Chapter 2, I suggested the Myers-Briggs Type Indicator to examine how you like to do things in the present. Now let's examine the past and future. In this chapter, I'll suggest strategies for reviewing your past and planning your future. Several times I'll ask you to write lists and then reflect on them.

Richard Bolles, in *The Three Boxes of Life*, described a study that was done on patients at a New York City hospital to see what made some patients heal faster than others after the same type of surgery. The researchers discovered that fast healers were those who believed there was some meaning to everything that happened to them, even if that meaning was not evident at the time of going through the experience.[1]

Such an attitude toward life is also helpful when you are well and considering major changes in your life. Meaning is a word with a slippery definition. It's an individual concept. My meaning will be different from yours. That's fine. It's just important that we both find some meaning in our lives.

If you can look back over your life and see a pattern that makes some sense to you, you feel secure, like you are on the right track. "People who have a sense of purpose are those who can take any random experience that happens to them and put it into some kind of larger perspective."[2] When you have a sense of purpose, you are more likely to find the courage to try new things, take on the next challenge. Lee Kaiser says, "Life can be viewed as an unfoldment process. This happened and this happened. What would be the next unfoldment? What would be the next logical step that seems to grow out of the past?"[3]

For example, when I moved to Florida in 1983, I decided to work on a PhD in Tampa. I lived in Orlando, so that meant driving 100 miles each way every week, spending 1 or 2 nights away from my family. I did the trek for three years and finished all the course work. In the last summer session, I turned in my proposal for my dissertation, which my professor and I had been working on for three months. He said, "I hope you will do this study sometime." I said, "Sometime! I thought this was my dissertation proposal." He said, "Well, I don't know if the committee will approve it." I walked out thinking, "How much longer can I jump through academic hoops?"

At the same time, my first consulting job with the American Management Association landed in my lap. The woman who was supposed to do it couldn't for personal reasons. My consulting career took off once I had worked for AMA, because it was very respected in the profession.

For several years I thought, "Why did I drive to Tampa for three years?" It all seemed such a waste. The answer that finally occurred to me was, "So I could learn to spend the night alone in a hotel and not be afraid." I do that all the time now, but the first time I did it I barely slept, because I was afraid. I didn't get what I thought I wanted, but while working toward it, I got something else that I wanted more. When I make sense of an unexpected turn in my life, I have more courage to try new things and am less likely to be thrown off or be unsettled by the next surprise. "Soren Kierkegaard wrote, 'Life can only be understood backward, but it must be lived forward.'"[4] When you have found some understanding about the past, you are more ready to move forward.

In the last chapter, I asked you to spend a considerable amount of time thinking about what you like to do and don't like to do. Now I'd like you to look back over the events of your past. The Howards, in *Exploring the Road Less Traveled*, said, "Most of us learn best, really learn, from our own experience—not simply from having things happen to us but from reflecting on what happens, both alone and in exchanges with others, so that the meaning of our experience becomes clear and we can make choices based on growing awareness rather than unchallenged assumptions."[5]

Reviewing Your Past

A way to reflect on what has happened to you is to do an exercise recommended by Ira Progoff in his Journal Workshops. List the steppingstones of your life—the significant events that have led you to where you are today.[6] Don't feel this has to be a definitive list or that it has to be in a correct order. Just quickly write the items as they occur to you. On another day, the list would be different.

Example of Steppingstones of a Physician

- Born 1943
- Decision to be a doctor 1956
- College 1961
- Medical School 1965
- Pediatric Residency 1969
- Married 1971
- Moved to Charlotte to begin practice 1972
- Children 1972 and 1975
- First full-time management position. CIGNA, Orlando, 1983
- Began consulting business 1988

Make your own list, using the work sheets at the end of the chapter. The old adage, "Those who do not study history are doomed to repeat it," applies to your personal history as well. After you've made your list, think about the following questions, writing your answers on the work sheets at the end of the chapter. The answers here are meant only for guidance. This, like all the exercises in this book, is an intensely personal experience

The examples of answers below are not connected to the list above. They are poingnant answers from a variety of clients I have worked with

- **What was good?** *I'm glad I became a surgeon. I've loved being able to quickly fix many problems.*
- **What was bad?** *Decision to invest money in so and so.*
- **What do you wish you had done?** *I wish I had become a history professor instead of going to medical school.*
- **What do you wish you had not done?** *I wish I had not divorced my first wife. In my third marriage, I'm still dealing with the same problems. I might as well have stayed in the first one and worked them out.*
- **Do you see some meaning or a pattern that makes sense to you?** *One person told me that, when he looked back at the past, he saw a pattern of leaving situations quickly when they became difficult (a marriage, a job). He wanted to not do that in this crisis. He wanted to take his time, think, move slower, sit with the pain a little longer, and perhaps make a better decision than some he had made in the past.*
- **Do you see a natural progression?** *A woman said she kept admiring men who were doing what she wanted to do. She realized she learned something from each of them, and now she is doing it.*

Answer the questions above for your own list of steppingstones, using the appropriate work sheets at the end of the chapter.

Often, we just keep living life at a breakneck speed without pausing to see what we can learn from what we have done. "[W]e want to work smarter rather than harder. Yet all of us are familiar with frantic busyness as a state that continually precludes us from opening to the quiet and contemplation it takes *to be* smart. The fast-moving mind rebels against slowing the pace because it intuits that it will not only have to reassess its identity but also take time to recover and recreate, and of course when we are in the buzzing-worker-bee mode, that would be a loss of momentum difficult to justify. We do not even have time to find out if our momentum is taking us over the nearest cliff."[7]

It is scary to slow down and process events, but the rewards can be great if you can sit with the uneasiness a little while. Progoff claims that to think about "the past periods of our lives gives us access to the unlived possibilities of our existence which the future may still give us an opportunity to fulfill, albeit in a different form."[8] Howard Figler, in *The Complete Job-Search Handbook*, says looking back at what you have done even allows you to get paid what you should. "Your ability to communicate your worth is a function of your ability to recognize value in your own experience and see how it can be translated into new capabilities."[9]

Planning Your Future

After you have thought about your present life, what you like to do and what you don't, and looked back at what has led you to where you are today, you are ready to set some goals for your future. List all of the things you want in your professional and private lives. Let your imagination run wild.

When you make the list, you may think all sorts of strange messages from the past: "I don't deserve it; I never really wanted it anyway; what about the starving, dying people who can't have what they want? You are getting too big for your britches." Either ignore or write the thoughts down, but keep on making the list. Barbara Sher, in *I Could Do Anything If I Only Knew What It Was*, says, "You can trust desire....There's a practicality in our longings that's beyond rational thought. Your desire will point you in the right direction better than any rules or well-meant advice."[10] Try to overcome the forces of resistance that keep you from thinking about what you really want in life. Write anything you desire, even if it is unreasonable, because no one else will know about it unless you choose to tell them.

Examples

- Continued happy marriage

- Financial security in retirement

- Fulfilling work

- Continued good health

- Able to resume competitive running

- Satisfying church life

- Kids will become happy, productive adults

- Make some impact on health care delivery, cost, service

Make your own list on the work sheets. After you've made an exhaustive list, pick one item that you would like to think more about. Write the answers to the following questions about that item on the work sheets at the end of the chapter. Again, the answers here are meant only for guidance.

- **What do you want?** Get out of clinical practice and into management.

- **What will you have to pay (sacrifice) to get it?** "The notion that you can simultaneously have it all is an illusion. Choices, sacrifices, and trade-offs are realities of life."[11] I need some experience and education. I may have to take a position that pays less than I get now in order to get experience.

- **What might get in the way, be an obstacle to getting what you want?** I live in a small town. There are no major clinics or hospitals that have or want medical directors. I may have to move.

- **Can you picture yourself already having it?** Write a paragraph describing yourself already having what you want. I am a good Vice President of Medical Affairs. I talk to physicians and administrators and try to get each to be patient with the other, to learn the art of compromising. I can tell physicians when they need to change behavior or practice patterns.

- **What one thing could you do today that would move you toward your goal?** You need short-, mid-, and long-term goals. Do something now to get you on the way. If a long-range goal is to be out of patient care and become a Vice President of Medical Affairs, find out what it takes to become chief of your clinical department or to get on the executive committee of your hospital. People who choose the VPMA career path have usually been heavily involved in the hierarchy of one or more hospital medical staffs.

- **What don't you want to do anymore?** Sometimes, if you can't figure out what you want to do, start with what you don't want to do. If you don't want to take night call anymore, how might you stop it? Can you pay someone else to take it? Can you take home less money to get out of it? Can you get more partners so you do it less often? Can you share call with a large group in town? Can you get out of clinical medicine?

- **What are your "Evil Secrets?"** This question "may help you clarify what you really want. One key to discovering what you really like and love is to ask yourself what are the things you don't like to admit. 'I don't like to admit it, but I need to be the center of attention.' O.K., find a career path that will let you show off. 'I don't like to admit it, but I don't like dealing with other people.' OK, then devise a role that will let you make your contribution through things done in your office, such as intellectual creativity and true technical superiority. 'I don't like to admit it, but I really want to be rich.' Fine, go out and build a business. 'I don't like to admit it, but I'm an intellectual snob.' That's all right, so find a career path that will allow you to work only with smart people. Play to your 'evil secrets.' Don't suppress them. You are a lot less flexible than you think."[12]

After you go through this exercise, you might want to explore in depth some other items from your want list by using the above questions. Extra work sheets are provided for expanding this exercise.

Monster Careers has another list of questions developed by James Gonyea that helps you dig even deeper to figure out what you like to do.[13] Answer these and see if the same themes keep emerging:

1. What subjects do you most enjoy reading about?
2. What television or radio programs do you most enjoy?
3. What are your favorite types of movies?
4. What are your favorite hobbies or pastimes?
5. What type of volunteer activities do you prefer?
6. What subjects do you enjoy discussing with friends?
7. What subjects come to mind when you daydream?

8. What have been your favorite jobs?

9. What were your favorite school subjects?

10. What are your pet peeves?

11. If you doodle, what do you often draw?

12. If you ran the world, what changes would you make?

13. If you won a million bucks, what would you do with it?

14. What are your favorite kinds of people?

15. How would you like to be remembered after your death?

16. What are your favorite toys?

17. How would you describe your political beliefs?

18. Whom do you most admire in life and why?

19. What tasks have brought you the most success?

20. What tasks do you think you could do well that you haven't yet done?

When you've been self-reflective as much as you want or need to be, make a list of the top three to five items you want to keep in mind. An insurance company in Hartford, Connecticut, did a national survey that showed that only three percent of Americans had written specific long-range goals.[14] "They may have long-range goals swimming around in their heads, but nothing's going to happen until they jerk those nebulous goals out of the air, plant them in the wet cement out there, come back to today, do their homework, and start controlling the only increment of time over which they have any control: Right now....An unwritten goal is merely a wish."[15]

If you write out a goal, your brain thinks it, your hand writes it, your eyes see it, and, then, your subconscious and the universe begin to plan ways to make it happen. If you keep your goals where you can see them each day, you can determine if you are truly spending your time trying to accomplish them or if you value other things more. If the latter is true, change your goals and be honest with yourself. "Once we can decide on what is really important and pay the price for it in time and effort, we can accomplish great things."[16]

Put these goals where you can see them. Spend some time thinking about them each day, but don't become obsessed with or overly worried about them. Just do one little thing each day that moves you toward your goal. Once, I wrote down some things I wanted and forgot about the list. I came across the list several years later and was amazed and pleased to find that I was doing three out of the five items. "It was Pasteur who said, 'Chance favors the prepared mind.' The more you have been trying to decide what to do about your work, the more likely you are to find a solution when you least expect it."[17]

"The greatest difficulties in getting what we want in life are, first, figuring out what we really want, and, second, taking the first step. By writing down your dreams and goals, you can learn what you want, and in what order of importance."[18]

We have to live in the paradox of wanting and delaying gratification. However, as Richard Bolles writes in *What Color is Your Parachute?* "You have got to know what it is you want, or someone is going to sell you a bill of goods somewhere along the line that can do irreparable damage to your self-esteem, your sense of worth, and your stewardship of the talents God gave you."[19] Want what you want, and then expect to work to get it—not that it will just be handed to you. Give yourself permission to make the list. Then pull back and be happy with what you have while working toward what you want. If you can stand the tension, you'll get more of what you want than do those who never stretch themselves to think about it. Without goals, you stagnate or go backward. With goals, you are drawn toward exciting possibilities. If you run out of things to strive for, you lose your zest for living.

References

1. Bolles, R. *The Three Boxes of Life*. Berkeley, Calif.: Ten Speed Press, 1981, p. 354.

2. Leider, R. *Life Skills: Taking Charge of Your Personal and Professional Growth*. San Diego, Calif.: Pfeiffer & Company, 1994, p. 121.

3. Kaiser, L., Kaiser and Associates, Brighton, Colo., personal communication, 1996.

4. Leider, R., *op cit.*, p. 23.

5. Howard, W., and Howard, A. *Exploring the Road Less Traveled*. New York, N.Y.: Simon and Schuster, Inc., 1985, p. 10.

6. Progoff, I. *At a Journal Workshop*. New York, N.Y.: Dialogue House Library, 1975, p. 102.

7. Whyte, D. *The Heart Aroused, Poetry and the Preservation of the Soul in Corporate America*. New York, N.Y.: Currency Doubleday, 1994, p. 99.

8. Progoff, I., *op. cit.*, p. 129.

9. Figler, H. *The Complete Job-Search Handbook*. New York, N.Y.: Henry Holt and Co., 1979, p. 231.

10. Sher, B., with Smith, B. *I Could Do Anything If I Only Knew What It Was*. New York, N.Y.: Bantam Doubleday Dell Publishing Group, Inc., 1994, p. 26.

11. Marion, P. *Crisis Proof Your Career*. New York, N.Y.: Berkeley Books, 1994, p. 49.

12. Maister, David H. *True Professionalism*. New York: The Free Press, 199. p. 34.

13. Taylor, J., with Hardy D. *Monster Careers*. New York: Penguin Books, 2004, p. 89.

14. Smith, H. *The 10 Natural Laws of Successful Time and Life Management*. New York, N.Y.: Warner Books, A Time Warner Company, 1994, p. 79.

15. *Ibid.*, pp. 82-83.

16. *Ibid.*, p. 105.

17. Figler, H., *op cit.*, p. 262.

18. Leider, R., *op. cit.*, p. 141.

19. Bolles, R. *The 1985 What Color is Your Parachute?* Berkeley, Calif.: Ten Speed Press, 1985, p. 82

Other Reading

Elbow, P. *Writing Without Teachers*. New York, N.Y.: Oxford University Press, Inc., 1973.

Work Sheets

Life Stepping Stones

My personal life stepping stones:

_____
_____
_____
_____
_____
_____

What was good about your stepping stones?

_____
_____
_____
_____
_____
_____

What was bad?

_____
_____
_____
_____
_____
_____

What do you wish you had done?

_____

_____

_____

_____

_____

What do you wish you had not done?

_____

_____

_____

_____

_____

Do you see some meaning or a pattern that makes sense to you?

_____

_____

_____

_____

_____

Do you see a natural progression?

_____

_____

_____

_____

_____

_____

Future Planning

Planning your future: What do you want from life?

1. _____

   _____

2. _____

   _____

3. _____

   _____

4. _____

   _____

5. _____

   _____

First Want

What do you want?

_____

_____

_____

_____

_____

_____

What will you have to pay (sacrifice) to get it?

_____

_____

_____

_____

_____

_____

What might get in the way, be an obstacle to getting what you want?

_____

_____

_____

_____

_____

_____

Can you picture yourself already having it?

_____

_____

_____

_____

_____

_____

What one thing could you do today that would move you toward your goal?

_____

_____

_____

_____

_____

_____

What don't you want to do anymore?

_____

_____

_____

_____

_____

_____

What are your "Evil Secrets?"

_____

_____

_____

_____

_____

Second Want

What do you want?

_____

_____

_____

_____

_____

What will you have to pay (sacrifice) to get it?

_____

_____

_____

_____

_____

What might get in the way, be an obstacle to getting what you want?

_____

_____

_____

_____

_____

Can you picture yourself already having it?

_____

_____

_____

_____

_____

What one thing could you do today that would move you toward your goal?

_____

_____

_____

_____

_____

What don't you want to do anymore?

_____

_____

_____

_____

_____

What are your "Evil Secrets?"

_____

_____

_____

_____

_____

Third Want

What do you want? What will you have to pay (sacrifice) to get it?

_____

_____

_____

_____

_____

What might get in the way, be an obstacle to getting what you want?

_____

_____

_____

_____

_____

Can you picture yourself already having it?

_____

_____

_____

_____

_____

_____

What one thing could you do today that would move you toward your goal?

_____

_____

_____

_____

_____

What don't you want to do anymore?

_____

_____

_____

_____

_____

What are your "Evil Secrets?"

_____

_____

_____

_____

_____

Fourth Want

What do you want?

_____

_____

_____

_____

_____

_____

What will you have to pay (sacrifice) to get it?

_____

_____

_____

_____

_____

_____

What might get in the way, be an obstacle to getting what you want?

_____

_____

_____

_____

_____

_____

Can you picture yourself already having it?

_____

_____

_____

_____

_____

What one thing could you do today that would move you toward your goal?

_____

_____

_____

_____

What don't you want to do anymore?

_____

_____

_____

_____

_____

_____

What are your "Evil Secrets?"

_____

_____

_____

_____

_____

_____

Fifth Want

What do you want?

_____

_____

_____

_____

_____

_____

What will you have to pay (sacrifice) to get it?

_____

_____

_____

_____

_____

_____

What might get in the way, be an obstacle to getting what you want?

_____

_____

_____

_____

_____

Can you picture yourself already having it?

_____

_____

_____

_____

_____

_____

What one thing could you do today that would move you toward your goal?

_____

_____

_____

_____

_____

What don't you want to do anymore?

_____

_____

_____

_____

_____

What are your "Evil Secrets?"

_____

_____

_____

_____

_____

Chapter Four

Planning for Change

When you finish life-work planning, you may decide to make some career changes. Sayings abound about people's resistance to change: "The only people who welcome change are wet babies." "Every change is perceived as a loss by someone." "You can't change others; you can only change yourself." These words of wisdom remind us that change is not easy. What we may dislike most is the sense of being out of control.

Some changes can be planned for. You can plan to change your career, move to another city, send your children to college, or buy a house. Other changes just come up and grab us, and then we learn to cope. You figure out how to survive the change of losing a loved one or being fired from a job. "Even moving from one management position to another level within the same company is a significant change and will carry with it all of the need for transitional adaptation, common to major personal crises."[1] One of the great challenges of life is not to let the vulnerability we feel when change surprises us keep us from seizing the power we have and planning for the future as much as we can.

We need to regain a sense of power and control in turbulent times and plan for the future. I don't mean control in the sense of bossing people around or arrogantly lauding our position over others to make them feel small. I'm talking about controlling our own destiny as much as we can. We need to use our personal power, not overuse or abuse our positional power, and not fret about power we do not have.

You can gain some sense of control over change by planning ahead and visualizing how the change will affect you. The more you can picture what you'd like to do the more you can make it possible.

"As you begin to negotiate change in your life, keep in mind that you're entitled to disorganization and confusion. They are signs of health. Sometimes they are the side-effects that make you resistant to a change, even though you earnestly want the final outcome."[2] Be patient with yourself and know the confusion will eventually subside and you will see the path clearer. "Changing can be a way of taking charge, of getting in the driver's seat, and of predicting your life's path while everything around you is unpredictable."[2]

In this chapter I'll discuss issues to think about if you are planning a career change and ways to continue what you are doing now but change your environment so you will be more satisfied.

Change Your Career

Before you make a career change, do some planning to make the transition go smoother. Think about the following issues:

Geography/Location

Where do you want to live? Is sunshine important to you or snow for cross country skiing? Do you like the wide open spaces of country living, or do you like to get to the grocery store or hardware store in five minutes? If the sight of miles and miles of cornfields gives you a feeling that all is right with the world, New York City will not be the place for you.

I like the tall trees, the rolling hills, and the brick houses where I grew up. I think we may be like baby ducks who choose as their mama the first animal they see. Our psyches tend to want to live in or get back to the kind of land we grew up in, if we had pleasant experiences there. Consider not fighting this urge—work on getting a job in the location you like best.

A couple from Arizona was interviewing for a job in the Northeast. The job, the schools, the house, the community all seemed right, but after two visits, something wasn't right, and they just couldn't figure it out. When they got back home, they realized the sun had not shone any time during their visits. They were used to seeing the sun every day, and they decided not to take the job. Sunshine was that important to them.[3]

Don't start with the notion that you will go anywhere in the country. You probably wouldn't be happy everywhere, and the thought is too broad to work with. Just as a history teacher told you to narrow your topic when you chose Russia as the subject for a term paper, pick a part of the country you like and then work to find a job there. If later, after a visit somewhere else, you decide the new place is all right, that's fine, but it's mind-boggling to start with the entire United States or the world in mind.

Health Issues

I have talked to people who have had a variety of health concerns. One person's arthritis improved in Arizona, but the dry weather there also caused another to suffer nosebleeds. One had circulation problems that worsened in extreme cold. Another's allergic reactions were continuous in the tropical warmth of Florida where something always blooms. Think about yourself and your family members. Will you be comfortable enough in the new location?

Life-Style

Life-style issues to consider are:

- Pace of life—Do you want to work from 8 a.m. to 6 p.m., or do you want to work from 6 a.m. to 9 p.m.? Many will say they do not have a choice. You always have choices. If two people drive a delivery truck and one works the night shift and the other the day shift, their life-styles are very different. Emergency department doctors and pediatricians have very different life-styles.

- Recreational opportunities—Do you want to play golf, sky dive, scuba dive, water or snow ski?

- Cultural events—Do you like opera, theater, ballet, foreign films?

- Social events—Do you want to belong to a country club, or do you prefer simple evenings at home with pizza and beer?

- Friends—In some areas, neighbors bring ice tea when you are unloading the moving van. In other areas, you can live there for years and never know your neighbor's name. Religion—Do you need a church, synagogue, mosque, or coworkers and neighbors who will accept your not wanting any of those structures?

Financial Needs

I once talked to a physician who made about six to ten thousand dollars a year. In addition, he received room and board where he worked. He said, "If I make much more than that, I give it away. He travels between Alaska, the Pacific Northwest, and Brazil throughout the year, giving his services away some of the time, making a modest salary other times. Variety, travel, and service to humanity are his most important values.

I talked to another physician who makes more than $400,000 and cannot get by on less. I am not asking you to pass judgment on yourself, but I am asking you to think hard about what amount you want and need and then make plans for how to get it.

Here are some questions to ask yourself:

- **What does it cost to live each month?** Make a list of the items.
   House payment
   Car payment
   Food
   Utilities
   Insurance
   Home repairs
   Recreation
   Savings for college
   Clothing
   Vacation
   Taking care of parent

- **What could you change?** Baber suggests that you then "categorize your monthly expenditures:

  Fixed: rent, mortgage, car payments, utilities

  Flexible: food, clothing, education, home improvements

  Frills: entertainment, club memberships, vacations[4]

  You probably can't change your house payment but could change clothes buying and recreation. A discussion of finances is often painful, because it kicks up a power struggle between partners—who decides how the money is spent. Is it shared equally? Should it be? Even though it is tough, make yourself talk about it. A fee-only financial planner, one who is selling nothing except advice, can be a big help, because he or she can help keep the conversation objective and give you advice without trying to sell you a product.

- **What amount of money do you have in a retirement fund?** What will it be worth when you retire? The time to begin planning your retirement finances is when you're young, when you have the years to build the "nest egg" you decide you'll need. If you desire an annual retirement income of $50,000, for instance, you'll need a fund of $715,000 to provide it without tapping the principal, presuming an interest rate of 7 percent.

  Some physicians want to keep working rather than retire, but I've talked to a number of physicians in their 60s who are having difficulty getting the jobs they want. Can you reduce your expenses when you retire? It would help if your house is paid for. "If you make even one extra mortgage payment a year, you can virtually cut a thirty-year mortgage in half—again, with big savings on interest."[5]

- **What do you make now? What will you make if you change jobs?** If you are going to step down in salary, can you try living on less for a couple of years to experience what it feels like and to build a financial cushion?

- **What severance benefits do you have and for how long?** Some people get as much as a full year of salary and benefits. Six months is nice. Three months is too little. Some organizations will not say they give severance, but many do if they fire you because they want to assuage their guilt, and they don't want you to talk too negatively about them.

- **What expenses can you anticipate for a job search?** "You will have new expenses during your job hunt: resume preparation, mailing, telephone, career counseling, health insurance, and memberships in professional associations if they previously were paid for by your employer."[6]

Experience

Organizations want medical directors who have experience. It's the age-old question of how do you get experience when everyone wants someone who already has experience. Volunteer to serve on and then lead committees on utilization review, quality assurance, patient safety, strategic planning, privileging, or credentialing. Become a department chair, president of the medical staff. Sometimes HMOs and insurance companies will hire physicians part time to do utilization review and quality assurance. See if that opportunity is available in your area.

Find someone who is doing what you want to do and talk to them about it. What experience led them to where they are? To get the job you want, you may have to take a less than ideal job to get some marketable experience. Chapter 5 is devoted to how to get experience.

Educational Needs

Think about what education you will need to do the job you want. You can learn management skills through courses from ACPE, other organizations, or master's degree programs. Which ones suit your time schedules, finances, study habits?

If you decide to get a master's degree, keep in mind that it will definitely help you do a management job, but it will not be an automatic guarantee that you will get a management job. When you finished your MD, you could go somewhere and immediately be a doctor. The same is not true for the master's degree programs. You will still need experience and contacts.

Culture Shock

"Once they move into management, physician executives find that their former associates in practice consider them 'traitors' who have left a 'real job' and abandoned membership in a select professional clique....They may find their social network of physician friends no longer interested in their company and aloof to them."[7]

Physicians have told me that when they move into management, they are neither fish nor fowl. Their physician colleagues think they are now one of the administrators, and the administrators think they are still one of the physicians. They cope with this isolation by getting together with other physician executives. A chief medical officer told me he gets together for dinner with five other CMOs in his area once a month. He said, "We are competitors, but also friends. We take off the gloves, talk about our problems, commiserate. We have no friends at our hospitals."

Several physician executives have formed organizations at the state or the local level. Many come to ACPE meetings primarily to be with like-minded people, and some keep in touch with other physician executives through regular phone calls.

Family Concerns

"Before signing on for a specific job, the physician should strongly consider the impact of this particular decision on the spouse and family. This includes issues such as relocation, a change in salary, uncertainty about the future, all of which could put great strain on family relationships. A physician executive is more likely to fail without good support from the 'home front.'"[8]

I have heard recruiters repeatedly talk about candidates who were well along in the search process and then dropped out because the spouse finally said, "I won't move." Once you have done that, a recruiter is not eager to present you in another search.

My husband was a practicing pediatrician who became more and more interested in medical management. He actively interviewed for positions for two years. Each time he went off to interview, I felt sick, because I did not want to leave Charlotte, North Carolina. I loved the town, my friends, the church, the schools; however, I knew I wouldn't be able to look at him years later and realize I kept him from doing something he had been working toward for so long. The city we lived in had only one large group and someone else had gotten that physician executive job. He interviewed in several places in the north and the Midwest for two years before an offer came from Florida. Having been reared in the South I preferred going to warmer weather rather than colder weather. I finally agreed to go.

Then I was miserable and resentful for a year. My husband was excited about the new job and the new set of friends at work. The children and I cried a lot, but after two months the children had adjusted. I became lonelier and angrier. I had given up a good job in Charlotte and was having trouble filling my days with meaningful activity. After a year had passed, we talked to a counselor to help us tell each other what we needed. If this happens to your family, go sooner. We finally got there, but my suffering might have been shortened had we gone sooner. You need a third party to help you tell each other what you want and how you hurt. The counselor can help make suggestions for what might make you feel better. It's hard to think of these things on your own when you are in the middle of much pain and frustration.

The second year in Florida, I began going to graduate school to work on a PhD. I've always loved going to school. The university was a 100 miles away so I spent the night and took all the classes I could get in that 24-hour period. I enjoyed getting away from home, child care, and cooking once a week, and I felt some sacrifices were being made on my behalf—that cures resentment.

You need to communicate with your family. Are they willing to move with you and perhaps more than once? There are no guarantees, but you have a better chance if everyone is talking about it. Explain how excited you are about management, about making a difference on a larger scale rather than in one-on-one patient care, about being a part of the solutions to health care reform. Or you may explain that the need for your specialty is drying up, and you are going to be without income. Listen long and hard to objections, whining, crying, complaining. That is part of the price of uprooting your family. Say you're sorry they're in pain. Offer to be with the children on Saturday or help with the baby sitting so your spouse can do something he or she wants to do. I know you are busy and keeping long hours, but you must find time and something of yourself to give—not just money—if you want more cooperation and less resentment.

Whether married or single, carefully consider what your obligations are. Whom do you need to take care of? Whom do you want to live close to?

Should You Resign?

I have met a fair number of physicians who want to leave their situations as fast as they can. Marion has a tough list of questions to ask yourself before you quickly leave what you are doing now:

- "Do you have enough money to live for six months while you look?

- "Are all the other areas in your life fairly stable: your marriage, your finances, your debt-to-savings ratio, your relationship with your children, your feelings about yourself?

- "Are your moods consistent?

- "Do you feel capable of structuring your day when there is little or no external structure?

- "Do you like working out of your house alone most of the day?

- "Do you feel okay knowing that this is a three-to-six-month effort requiring six to eight hours a day?

- "Do you have supportive friends to help you through this process?

- "Do you have a network of 125 or more colleagues, friends, and co-workers or have what it takes to build one?

- "Do you have some good answers as to why you resigned?

- "Do you feel confident enough to handle the barrage of questions from recruiters, employers, and colleagues?

"If you can answer yes to most or all of these questions, it may be that you have sufficient structure in your life to go on your own. In this case, you may want to resign and work full time on your crisis-proof career."[9]

Change Your Environment

If you decide you can't leave your situation, changing your environment may help. You may decide you do not want to make a dramatic career change, but you want to make changes in your life so you are more satisfied. You do have choices in life. Even if you continue to do exactly what you are doing professionally, you have the choice of changing your attitude about it, of adding pleasurable experiences to your life, of reducing your work load so you have time for recreation. You need to ask yourself, "What plans can I (or have I) formulated to reduce...stress (e.g., exercise program, more sleep, more time off)?"[10] If you died tomorrow, life would go on somehow, so you might as well take some time off. If it means less money, what expenses could you cut back on to make that possible?

Pick one or two of the following to try. Schedule more free time or take up a new hobby. Take art, dance, or music classes. Help the homeless. Watch the Comedy Channel. Join a group that believes in a cause. Get a pet that will be affectionate and accept you as you are all the time.

Make time for exercise. You've heard that over and over again. If you are still not doing it, keep trying to make it happen. You simply cannot have a sense of well-being without exercise. The body was made to move, and if it doesn't get to, your mind, body, and spirit will suffer. Exercise can make you have or regain a sense of power. Slamming a golf ball far down the fairway can restore your feeling of control over some things. Running or walking fast gives you energy, releases frustration, and makes your body feel strong and slim.

Talk to Someone

Talk it over with someone, preferably a counselor. "You should seek professional intervention (such as psychotherapy) any time you become entrenched in a personal issue that is so intense or of such long duration that it affects your career....You don't have to be on the verge of a nervous breakdown to ask for help. A few short sessions may help you get unwedged."[11]

Family members eventually get worn out with the topic of your frustrations about health care changes and about career changes that you are considering. Also, they may feel frightened by these losses, so you may hold back some of your discontent. "The most resistance to switching jobs (or careers) often comes from colleagues or members of one's family who may feel threatened by a proposed change."[12]

A physician told me he would be ruined if he talked to a counselor. His insurance company would not cover him anymore if it learned he had had mental health counseling. If you worry about such repercussions, try a minister or a wise friend. Another option is to pay for these services yourself and not charge them to your insurance carrier. Some big group practices have private employee assistance programs just for their physicians. The CEO, who might insist that the physicians use the service, does not know what happens when they do. In many cases, the situations are improved and the process is completely confidential, and that is the CEO's only concern.

Separate whether you dread most how the change will affect you or how others will react to it. Will your spouse and children make you miserable because you are bringing in less money? How can you talk about it? Is there anything that can be done? Can you cut back on expenses? You might say to your family, _____ is happening. We have to cut back somewhere." Does everyone give up something or do you determine who gives up what? Often, it can't be a democratic family vote. Perhaps you decide a daughter must give up riding lessons or a son golf lessons. A teenager might get an afternoon job to finance some of the extras.

Find a support group—like-minded people who want to do an activity that you want to do or who want to complain about and problem solve issues that matter to you. Do you have people you can talk to about your life? For some, one on one is desirable. Others need a group to be with. Carl Jung, a late 19th and early 20th Century psychiatrist and philosopher, said that, for the well-balanced life, we need to tend to the inner and the outer life, but neither to the exclusion of the other. We can examine our inner selves when we are working or thinking alone, but we need a group or a community as a context for tending to the outer life. We need to interact with others, come up against their needs and wants, and use the energy of many ideas to get things done. Working with others in some way helps our own lives be centered, productive, healthy.

Write about It

You can tend to the inner life by writing in a journal for 10 minutes a day. You can write out some of these anxieties. Choose paper and pen you like or a computer and write 10 minutes a day, five days a week without worrying about spelling, grammar, or punctuation. Just start writing and don't stop for 10 minutes, whether you think you have anything to write about or not.

Write about the injustice of all the changes in health care. Lambaste the legal profession, government regulations and cuts, the new electronic medical record, ungrateful patients, whatever is causing longer hours and less money. When you do this kind of writing, you may touch on subjects that surprise you and that you wouldn't ever want anyone to see. If that happens, tear up the paper it is written on. You don't have to keep it to have the process benefit you. As Peter Elbow says, "Garbage in your head will poison you, but garbage on paper can safely be put in the wastepaper basket."[13] A physician recently took this suggestion and called to tell me he does the writing at the end of the day, and he has started sleeping better at night.

References

1. Hartfield, J. "Career Paths." In *Physicians in Managed Care. A Career Guide.* Bloomberg, M., and Mohlie, S., Editors. Tampa, Fla.: American College of Physician Executives, 1994, p. 72.

2. Wonder, J., and Donovan, P. *The Flexibility Factor.* New York, N.Y.: Ballantine Books, 1989, p. 6-7.

3. Bonfield, W. "It Took a Distant Opportunity to Show Us We Like It Where We Are." *Physician Executive* 14(5):8-11, Sept.-Oct. 1988

4. Baber, A., and Waymon, L. *How to Fireproof Your Career. Survival Strategies for Volatile Times.* New York, N.Y.: Berkley Books, 1995, p. 125.

5. *Ibid.*, p. 139.

6. *Ibid.*, p. 125.

7. Peters, R. *When Physicians Fail As Managers.* Tampa, Fla.: American College of Physician Executives, 1994, p. 14.

8. *Ibid.*, p. 38.

9. Marion, P. *Crisis Proof Your Career.* New York, N.Y.: Berkley Books, 1994, pp. 164-5.

10. *Ibid.*, p. 133.

11. *Ibid.*, p. 57.

12. Leider, R. *Life Skills.* San Diego, Calif.: Pfeiffer and Company, 1994, p. 83.

13. Elbow, P. *Writing Without Teachers.* London, England: Oxford University Press, 1973, p. 8.

Other Reading

Alexander, J. *Dare to Change*. New York, N.Y.: New American Library, 1984.

Covey, S. *The 7 Habits of Highly Effective People*. New York, N.Y.: Simon and Schuster, 1989.

Frankl, V. *Man's Search for Meaning*. New York, N.Y.: Washington Square Press, 1985. (First published in 1946.)

Gillett, R. *Change Your Mind. Change Your World*. New York, N.Y.: Simon and Schuster, 1992.

Seagrave, A., and Covington, F. *Free from Fears*. New York, N.Y.: Poseidon Press, 1987.

Wallen, E. "Job Pressures Seen Fueling Rise in Doctors' Stress Levels." *Physicians Financial News*, Oct. 15, 1993, pp. 15-16

Wheelis, A. *How People Change*. New York, N.Y.: Harper-Colophon Books, 1973.

Work Sheets

Personal Parameters of a Career Change

Geography/Location (list all of the conditions that you would impose on a move from your present location):

_____

_____

_____

_____

_____

_____

_____

Health Issues (list considerations for all members of your family):

_____

_____

_____

_____

_____

_____

_____

Life-Style (include, but do not limit yourself to, pace of life, recreational opportunities, cultural events, social events, and friends):

_____

_____

_____

_____

_____

_____

_____

Financial Needs

Monthly Costs:

House payment _____

Car payment _____

Food _____

Utilities _____

Insurance _____

Recreation _____

Savings for college _____

Clothing_____

Vacation_____

Taking care of parents _____

Other _____

Other _____

Other _____

Other _____

Other _____

Total_____

What would you change? (categorize your monthly expenses)

Fixed   _____

                 _____

                 _____

                 _____

Flexible   _____

                 _____

                 _____

                 _____

Retirement funds (list current funds and projected funds for anticipated retirement years. In constructing a financial retirement package, remember that you will want to live on the interest on your retirement fund principal. For instance, the annual income at 7 percent interest on a fund of $715,000 is $50,000. If you will require more income, the principal must be increased by $143,000 for each income increase of $10,000.):

Current funds   _____

Funds ____ years from now   _____

Funds ____ years from now   _____

Funds ____ years from now   _____

Funds ____ years from now   _____

Funds ____ years from now   _____

Anticipated salary in new job   _____

Severance and other benefits (amount and term)

_____   _____

_____   _____

_____   _____

_____   _____

_____   _____

Job Search Expenses

Resume preparation _____

Mailing and shipping_____

Telephone _____

Career counseling _____

Health insurance _____

Membership dues_____

Other _____

Other _____

Other _____

Other _____

Checklist for Resignation (if you respond positively (Y) to most of these questions, you can probably sustain yourself and your family for the six months or so needed to find another position. Otherwise (N), hunt from where you are)

◆ Do you have enough money to live for six months while you look?_____

◆ Are all the other areas in your life fairly stable: your marriage, your finances, your debt-to-savings ratio, your relationship with your children, your feelings about yourself? _____

◆ Are your moods consistent?_____

◆ Do you feel capable of structuring your day when there is little or no external structure?_____

◆ Do you like working out of your house alone most of the day?_____

◆ Do you feel okay knowing that this is a three-to-six-month effort requiring six to eight hours a day?_____

◆ Do you have supportive friends to help you through this process?_____

◆ Do you have a network of 125 or more colleagues, friends, and co-workers or have what it takes to build one?_____

◆ Do you have some good answers as to why you resigned?_____

◆ Do you feel confident enough to handle the barrage of questions from recruiters, employers, and colleagues?_____

Chapter Five

What Do You Have to Do
to Become a Physician Executive?

Physicians who are considering moving from clinical practice into management often ask, "What do you have to do to make the change?"

Become a board-certified clinician who practices three-five years.

Residents who are interested in management and who do not want to practice clinically have asked, "Why do I need to be board-certified when I am not going to practice?" As a medical director (VPMA, CMO) you will be working with physicians, in some cases telling them what they can and cannot do. Physicians respect other physicians most for their knowledge of disease and their capacity to take care of patients. Only gradually do they come to respect them for their management skills. They will not take instructions from someone who has not had to cope with an overcrowded schedule, shrinking resources, government regulations, the threat of malpractice suits, and night call, to name a few of the frustrating realities of being a practicing clinician.

Get management experience.

Serve on and then lead committees and task forces. When something needs to be done, raise your hand and volunteer to do it. Let people see you doing management activities, working with people and tackling problems.

George Linney, MD, an executive search consultant for Tyler and Company, says, "Become a department chair. Serve on significant committees, such as:

- Cost containment
- Quality
- Performance improvement
- IT implementation
- Credentialing (an important function but not earth shaking)
- By-laws committee (significant if you are upheaving the organization. If you are doing it just to show the Joint Commission that you have done it, it is not that significant).

"How do you do this?

"Volunteer to take the lead in transformation to EMR. Say, 'I know how to do this, and I'll get all surgeons to do it next year. Here's how we are going to do it.' Start with departments where you sense there is going to be less resistance—maybe one that has more young physicians in it who just finished residency. Then move through age groups. Or you might do radiology first because radiologists are more into electronics. Most of them have figured out how to transmit CAT scans, x-rays, and MRIs electronically. If someone is in a wreck, the MRI and CAT scan are often sent to the radiologist's house for interpretation. The radiologist sends back oral and written interpretations. His or her part of the EMR is already done.

"What you call a person who volunteers to do this is a 'champion.' The VPMA may also be the champion, but in a big system he/she can't do it alone. You don't have to be a computer whiz. You just learn what you need to know and pull the other folks along."

Get involved in the county medical society, the state medical society, the American Medical Association. Some HMOs and insurance companies hire people to do utilization review and quality assurance part time. This is valuable experience for a management career.

"If you think you might be interested in hospital management, you would be wise to do what you can to move up in the elected or selected hierarchy of your hospital medical staff. Express interest in becoming chair of your clinical department or be willing to serve on the hospital executive committee. Be available to take a job as an elected officer of the hospital staff. The same would be true for those aspiring to positions in management in medical group practices or various types of HMOs."[1]

I knew a Florida physician who had been part of a team that was planning a state HMO. He said that, if you had asked him six months earlier if he would be involved in such a project, he would have said no. Some physicians helped with the formation of physician-hospital organizations and then, when that trend changed, they helped the hospital sever those ties. You might volunteer to work with your hospital or group practice on electronic medical records, computerized physician order entry, patient safety initiatives, or outcomes monitoring projects.

Many men and women go into management in the middle of their careers. They may reach the point where they feel they have done all the cardiovascular surgery they want to do, or they can't discuss otitis media one more time. It is no longer a challenge, and they need a new challenge. Because many people come to the point in their careers where they want a change, it is a good idea to volunteer for committees throughout your career to continually learn new activities, make yourself visible in the organization, and have experience to put on your resume should you decide some day that management appeals to you.

You may have to take a management job that is not quite right in order to get the necessary experience. Once you go into the management arena, you may have to move every three to five years. You need to think about whether you want to do that.

Get education.

The Physician in Management seminars of the American College of Physician Executives are an excellent source of training in basic management skills. Attend the College's Institutes, which have even more concentrated areas of study. Be on the alert for informal educational opportunities from other national professional organizations and from local colleges and universities. Increasingly, it is important to have a master's degree if you want to be a serious candidate presented by a recruiter.

Find a mentor.

Roger Schenke, ACPE Executive Vice President, advises: "Find yourself a mentor—male or female. Someone who has experience, who will help you think. Look for someone who is an effective person. If you admire the person and think you would like to be more like him or her, try to get on a committee that the person is on, or in an educational program that the person is in. Get in the same room, get to know the person. It will be natural for the conversation to be around management issues. Then ask: 'How does someone get involved in management in this organization? How did you get to where you are? Has this management change been good for you? What education did you get?' If that person sees you begin to do management activities, he or she becomes like your mother or father, because he or she helped to get you started."[2]

Mentoring takes less time than many people think. The person does not have to be in your organization or even in your town. You can call them and say, "Can you listen to me for a while? 20-30 minutes."

Mentoring does not have to be regular. I have heard people try to set up formal situations—a contract where I'll help you with your weakness and you help me with mine. Once in a while that might work, but a formal commitment to a specific amount of time can scare people off. They may give you that much time because they get interested in you, but they don't want to promise it.

In some organizations, mentoring situations exist where someone spends a considerable amount of time at another location—at another hospital in the same hospital system or at another staff model in the same managed care system. A new medical director can be sent to the site and walk around with an experienced medical director for a week and learn how he or she does things.

Linney says, "Information interviews are valuable and may be the beginning of a mentoring relationship. They can be done in person on or the phone. There are two types. First, you can have an information interview with a physician in management who has a job that you think you would like. For instance, if you are interested in group practice management, interview several physicians who are medical directors in group practices. These information interviews may lead to a long-term mentor relationship."[1]

"A second type of information interview would be one in which you interview someone who works for an organization that you might like to work for. If you desire an information inter-view with a health care executive in a large insurance company, plan two or three questions that you would ask that person and tell them ahead of time that you do not intend to take more than 15 minutes of his or her time. You should have the key questions written out so you could at least get them answered if there is not time to get other questions dealt with. Of course, if you already know the person, it would be all right to expect a longer interview or possibly an interview over lunch that you pay for."[1]

Don't continue a mentoring relationship if sexual stuff gets in the way. It is very natural for people who work together to become good friends. The sparks of creativity generated by good minds thinking together can sometimes lead to sexual thoughts. If either person acts on these thoughts, it is wise to end a mentoring relationship. The trouble you can get into can outweigh any benefits you might receive.

Kaiser says, "[W]e are all mentors for the people who have not moved as far on the path as we have, and at the same time we are dependent on mentors who are further along on the journey to help us take the next step....You may never be able to help the people who help you. Your service is to those who are coming along behind you."[3]

You can also gather information from books and seminars. *Essentials of Medical Management*, *Positive Leadership in Healthcare*, and *Physician Executives: What Why and How*, all published by ACPE, describe medical management issues. Cheryl Richardson, a life coach, said, "Often when I finished a book that had a great impact on me, I made a point to look for a workshop led by the author."[4] Many of the authors of the above books teach ACPE courses.

The Physician in Management Seminar, live or on CD, discusses an overview of manage-ment topics. Attending some live courses gives you a chance to talk to other physician exec-utives and get information from them first hand on what they do and on the career path that led them to it.

ACPE's on-line networks allow physician executives to keep in touch by email in between meetings. The VPMA network always has a vigorous discussion going on. People ask any kind of clinical and management question and get some suggestions in a few hours or days. ACPE has an advisor/mentor service that connects you by phone or email with advisors who might become mentors if the chemistry is right.

How Some Physician Executives Gained Experience

Peters describes the dual nature of the physician executive's role. "The job dimensions of physician managers...are of a 'clinical' nature—evaluating physician performance, utiliza-tion and case review, recruiting physicians and defining their clinical activities, and quality of care considerations. Other tasks are of a more 'managerial' nature—planning, budgeting, marketing, and cost of care considerations."[5] You will need experience in both areas before you can get a full-time position.

I interviewed four physician executives and asked them how they got the experience that led to their management careers.

Gregory Taylor MD, MSHA, FACPE, CPE
Medical Director, High Point Regional Health System, High Point, NC

"I worked in the Emergency Department from 1982 to 1993 at Mary Washington Hospital in Fredericksburg, Virginia. I looked innovatively at the ED in terms of patient flow, turn-around times, patient satisfaction. We were doing a lot of recruitment, getting into the controversial issues about credentialing—who would get to do what. We started new programs—a neonatology service with an NICU. We recruited a neurosurgeon and were laying the foundation for an open heart program. We were actively involved in building the new hospital, planning, bonds. I became department chair, then vice chief of staff, and then chief of staff.

"Mary Washington was small enough that we couldn't justify a CMO or a VPMA. Essentially the chief of staff filled that role. In 1990 I gave up a third of my clinical time to become chief of staff, and they paid me $40,000. That didn't make up for the income I lost giving up my clinical practice, but it made it doable. I was not aware of many folks that were paying that kind of money for the chief of staff 13-14 years ago.

"In 1992 my wife and I took a very long walk on the beach and I told her I wanted to make a career change, and I wanted to go back to school. She was very supportive. She said, "Do it now while the children are in 5th and 6th grade. There is never going to be a better time." I enrolled in MCVs master's program—two weeks on campus a semester. The rest was electronic format, but imagine the Internet in 1992. We had physicians, pharmacists, physical therapists, nurses—a very diverse class, which was wonderful in terms of interaction.

"I also started job hunting at that point. I saw a job posted in the *Physician Executive Journal*. I contacted Tyler and Co. I went for an interview in the winter of '93 and moved to Cape Fear Valley Health Center in the summer. I was their first VPMA. It was 500 beds. We purchased Columbia's HCA hospital, so when I left it was an 800-bed system. I was there 11 years.

"In January 2004, I moved to a new city and became the Chief Medical Officer of High Point Regional Health System."

Donald A. Pocock, MD, FACP, CPE
Chief Medical Officer, Morton Plant Mease Health Care, Clearwater, FL

"I had gone through the whole ACPE program before I took a management position. As our group got bigger, I realized there was not a physician member who had formal business training. When we got beyond 25 doctors, it got harder to handle the different personalities, the strategic planning and the finances. I was the one in the group who dealt with scheduling, conflict resolution, educating people on how to code, how to be in compliance with the federal guidelines as far as charging levels and documentation issues. In the hospital I had chaired utilization review and credentials committees for a number of years. I was Chief of Medicine for ten years, then Vice Chief of Staff, then Chief of Staff and then served on the Board.

"The VPMA left and, so I assumed that role on a day-to-day basis for six months. I was offered the job full time but decided I really didn't want to do it in that town. I had been there for 21 years, had a lot of history. I decided to go somewhere new to become a VPMA.

"I got a job in Charleston and was there for four years. They had never had a VPMA. The docs wanted someone they could control, and the CEO wanted someone who was independent. In four months, the CEO was fired.

"Then I had an interim CEO for 14 months and then a CEO who came out of the Tenent system so I had 3 bosses in four years. The senior staff had changed a good bit. There was not a solid team that I felt close to. The position wasn't as fulfilling as I wanted it to be.

"I heard about a position in Florida. I had known the VPMA. We had worked together at the state level a couple of times. When I heard he had been promoted to the Quality Chief and the VPMA position opened up, I called the recruiter doing the search. She didn't remember me, but we had talked a couple of years before. I sent her my resume. She talked to the VPMA, who gave me a good endorsement. Between the two I got offered an interview. It was one of those interviews that just clicked from the moment you walked in and sat down. I was offered the job."

Susan Freeman MD, MS, CPE, FACPE
Chief Medical Officer, Temple University Hospital, Philadelphia, PA

"I was in a small private practice for three years before I became the endocrinology chair in a 215-member multispecialty faculty practice affiliated with the University of Minnesota. It merged with Health Partners in the '90s. Then I became the Endocrinology Department chair of the whole citywide Health Partner's system with multiple offices. I was also medical director for quality for the ambulatory clinics during that time.

"I knew that if I positioned myself well, I could be instrumental in the merger. Many of my colleagues decided to leave, but I decided to dive in head first. I became Medical Director of Quality in our ambulatory clinic. I got my master's degree at University of Wisconsin Madison. Then I became VPMA of the hospital. The merger helped that happen quickly. I was with that organization for 8 years.

"Then I worked as medical director for a venture capital company. It was a health benefit designed plan. I worked to get its case management and disease management programs up and going.

"Then I became VPMA in Connecticut. Even though the title was the same, the job was much different. It had more operations and profit and loss responsibilities with the centers of excellence at the hospital. Example: I was responsible for making sure that the cardiology center ran well, was capturing adequate market share, and was bringing in appropriate revenue. You do studies, you evaluate volume and where the people are coming from and who is referring them. Then you do marketing and you target those physicians or regions that are not referring as many patients as you would like."

Alan S. Kaplan MD, MMM, CPE, FACPE
Vice President, Chief Medical Officer & Operations, Edward Health Services Corporation
Naperville, IL

"I was a chief resident and left there for private practice in an ER group. I wanted to do more. I wanted to be on committees. There was no opportunity there for me so the group made up a position—co-chair of occupational medicine. There was no job description, no accountabilities, no expectations. I got paid well to do nothing. When I look back on it, it is almost an embarrassment. I'm not sure they thought it was made up, but I did.

"I had been there 3½ years, making a lot of money, when I got a call that an emergency department in Naperville, Illinois, was looking for a new medical director. There were three internal candidates with a lot of talent, but the CEO decided at the interview that I was the person she wanted regardless of my background. The job was 50% clinical and 50% administrative.

"I was a bundle of energy and ideas. I went to task. My high energy and naivete played to my favor. As soon as I got in here, I noticed that the occupational medicine program was awful. Patients were complaining. Staff were complaining. Doctors were a pain in the butt. The general medical staff would come in, rotate and do corporate physicals. They would always be late, not follow up on tasks. Knowing what didn't work in my previous position, I immediately decided—I am going to hire the best occupational doctor I can. I am going to bring this in-house, and we are going to create a first-class program that meets the needs of our clients.

"Overnight I built a new occupational program and never included the medical staff. They went ballistic. The orthopedists didn't like it. I was controlling referrals. The primary care physicians couldn't subsidize their practices anymore doing physicals. It was a very bad situation for a little while. My CEO was quite amused by the way I went about this, was quite supportive, and we just lived through the politics. I had a lot of discussions with the medical staff. I ate crow. Said I'm sorry. Everything calmed down. I learned from it, and the program flourished.

"What it did for me was that the CEO said, "I think Alan can do a little more than just run the ER." She asked if I would be the physician champion for the business plan to create an urgent care center five miles to the south. I had a business planner that did the plan, but I understood the medical part of it. Even though I had no operations experience at that point, we developed the urgent care center over six months and got it fully staffed. That accomplishment was not controversial.

"I had a lot of passion. I was on call 24/7. If I saw a quality issue, I'd address it; a medical staff problem, I'd address it. I was always available. I didn't take vacations at that time in my life. I was a good clinician, so the medical staff respected me for that aspect. I had a wife and young babies. I only lived 3 miles from work. My wife was very tolerant.

"In my early years, I was that physician hitting the glass ceiling. I wished people would come to me for a business problem. They always came to me because they had a sore throat. I am a big fan of ACPE. A transition occurred when I went out to seek my own education, did a lot of course work, got the MMM. I worked very hard not to irritate people with my new education. I tried to learn from others whenever I could. Something happened after the MMM, but before I got the position I have now, people started coming to me with business issues. It was at that transition that we had a little shakeup of our administration. The CEO looked at me and says—just over night—'You've got ISS (Information System Services) and materials management, have fun.'

"I got these instant successes and they had no VPMA at the hospital, so the president said, "Lets have Alan start coming to the senior staff meetings and see how it goes." Within a few months she offered me a position as Vice President of Hospital-Based Physicians, which she quickly changed to VPMA because that was the vogue term at the time.

"I was lucky enough to get that first opportunity. Once I got it, I attacked it with passion. My focus was the 34,000 patients that walked through the ER. Early on I had to fire a lot of doctors. I cleaned out one third of that department and brought in new people, changed compensation systems, kept good people. Eleven years and 35 doctors later, I have had only two voluntary turnovers—that's it. I never use a recruiter to recruit physicians. Now those operations see 65,000 in the ER, 30,000 in the immediate care center, and 28,000 in the occupational health department. I grew the visits from 34,000 in the ER in the beginning to in excess of 100,000 in three areas today. The ER is the most profitable service line in the hospital. The key is that, early on in my career, I always had a focus on community and the right thing to do and that drove my decisions.

"I would say to my peers, 'When you are passionate about something, you attack things with goals. When you attack things with goals, they lead to accomplishments. When you get accomplishments, you get promoted. As opposed to you just want the position because you like the income and the status and want to make friends—you get experience but you don't get accomplishments."

Having presented the ways in which these four physician executives got their experience, I want to end this chapter with a wish list that an organization gave to a recruiter for the qualities it wanted in its next medical director. Organizations want physician executives to have experience handling the problems associated with the many changes in health care, but they also want strong communication skills, which will be discussed in the next chapter.

1. We need someone who will not say one thing and do another.

2. The medical director must help us understand where administration stands on various issues.

3. The person must demonstrate consistency and fairness.

4. The physician must have the ability to stand up to special selfish interests on the medical staff. (e.g., orthopedists who won't take trauma call even when the by-laws are clear on that issue.)

5. The medical director will help us with all the transitional stress, such as personnel needs, downsizing, consolidation of medical staffs.

6. The person will develop managed care agreements that protect all parties.

7. We still have lots of room for improvement in reducing lengths of stays.

8. The person must be strong on quality.

9. The medical director must have significant managed care experience, but that is not as important to us as the willingness to learn that stuff and teach it to us.

10. Some doctors feel that they are being told what to do by administration. If the medical director can break down some of that feeling, he or she will win a lot of points.

11. If the medical director can help us deal with some of our problem staff members, he or she will gain credibility right away.

12. More important to us than technical skills are personal traits—warm and friendly, a diplomat, a good communicator (by that we mean someone who is good at listening, explaining, and convincing).

References

1. George E. Linney Jr., MD, CPE, FACPE, Vice President, Tyler & Company, Atlanta, Georgia, personal communication, 2006.

2. Roger Schenke, Executive Vice President, American College of Physician Executives, Tampa, Florida, personal communication, 2006.

3. Kaiser, L. *Lifework Planning*. Brighton, Colo.: Brighton Books, 1989, p. 7.

4. Richardson, C. *The Unmistakable Touch of Grace*. New York, N.Y.: Free Press, 2005, p. 59.

5. Peters, R. *When Physicians Fail as Managers*. Tampa, Fla.: American College of Physician Executives, 1994, p. 6.

Chapter Six

What Communication Skills
Have You Needed Most in Your Job?

I asked experienced physician executives what communication skills have been most useful in their management positions. In this chapter you will read their responses and then a discussion of the most needed communication skills.

Gregory Taylor MD, MSHA, FACPE, CPE
Medical Director, High Point Regional Health System High Point, NC

"The ability to listen, talk to people one-on-one, and understand where physicians are coming from. I have an undergraduate degree in psychology and most days I wish I had a PhD in it. I spent my first two years in High Point trying to build a communication process with our medical staff.

"I did a physician satisfaction survey. Three areas of concern were communication, leadership, and responsiveness. We were in the 67th percentile, but we said, 'We are going to get to the 90th percentile.' Then we did an individual communication profile. We said, 'Here are some ways we can communicate with you. What is your preference? Newsletters, regular mail, faxes, email, internally electronically via our physician portal where physicians get on line to check their labs, Mercury MD where they download labs to their PDAs.' About half said, 'I like mail, faxes, newsletters. I don't know how to do email.' The other half said, 'I'm electronic, I'm young, email me, use list serves, blog me.' Our challenge is separating those two divisions.

"To improve communication :

- We produce quarterly audio newsletters on CDs that tell what is happening. They are messages from myself, chief of staff, vice chief of staff, CEO and chief nursing officer. Examples of topics: Joint Commission is coming this year. Here's what you need to know about it. We are going to do another satisfaction survey—we want your input. The chief nursing officer talks about the new performance coaches that were part of their response to the communication issue.

- We go meet with individual physicians at their offices any time at their convenience.

- Every week the vice president on call makes rounds with the physicians. It's not just me. There are 10 of us. In critical care, unit nurses would be included but, for the most part, it is a one-on-one interaction with the physician. I was just in the ICU with one of our intensivists. I make a strong effort to say, 'What can we do to make your practice easier, to improve patient safety? Are there any systems issues we can help with that you have identified?'

- Train performance coaches. When nurses looked at the survey, they found physicians did not know who to go to on the unit when they had concerns. If they felt a patient wasn't being turned adequately or got the wrong medication, they didn't know whom to tell. We redefined and recreated the old charge nurse position and have named them performance coaches. They have two primary purposes. One is to mentor, train and be a resource for the nursing staff but also to be the primary source of communication with our physicians when they have concerns.

- Confront disruptive behavior. We just passed a new code of conduct policy for physicians. It stipulates that there will be a joint investigation by the chief of staff and myself if there is an incident of disruptive behavior. It is rare here. We have an excellent nursing staff. We are a magnet facility. Tenure is unbelievable. Many members of the nursing staff have been here 20-30 years. There are not a lot of the traditional turf issues, immaturity and people who get defensive. The immediate past chief of staff, the chief of staff, and the chief of staff-elect are perfect role models. They are wonderful physicians, great human beings, and perfect gentlemen. I couldn't imagine any one of those three being obnoxious to any of our staff. We are very fortunate.

- Strive for excellence. As the final response to the communication issues, the administrators have adopted the Malcolm Baldrige criteria as the way we are going to manage this facility. From our CEO to our management team, we have gotten the organization energized about being good, but we want to be the best.

"My CEO agreed to support me to become an examiner for the Baldrige program. It is the most exciting thing I have ever done professionally. You commit to a week in Washington for training. I went on a site visit last year to an organization similar to ours. It was a mature organization that is trying to do many of the things we are trying to do so to see it first hand was great. Also the organization employs two thirds of its medical staff, which is a model that fell out of favor for a while but is coming back in vogue. They have been doing it for many years out in the cornfields of Wisconsin."

Donald A. Pocock, MD, FACP, CPE
Chief Medical Officer, Morton Plant Mease Health Care, Clearwater, FL

"Being an internist for my entire professional career helped because you have to be a listener. One of the problems we can get into is speaking too quickly and forming decisions before we have all the information. Having the ability to both write and speak on your feet is critical. A lot of people can write well but they stumble when they get up in front of an audience. You are always on stage in this job. You are always being watched for a variety of reasons. You have to be able to present yourself as confident and calm. You can't be afraid to take a position and stand up to folks, but at the same time you have to do it in a very controlled fashion. If you respond too quickly, you will lose your credibility.

"Two nights ago I had a conference with a guy who was throwing charts and was verbally abusive. I had the first conversation with him about a week earlier telling him we were going to have a sit-down session. Then I had the Department of Medicine chair with me when we met. We basically just listened and then I said, 'I appreciate all the things you are telling me about your frustration. This is not about that. This is about your behavior. I understand that you became frustrated. There are better ways to express that. This is the only warning you are going to get. The next time you are going to be suspended.' He calmed right down.

"Writing. You are always doing something for your boss. You are doing letters for him that he is going to put out or you are summarizing situations for him. We are dealing, as many places are, with the demand for pay for call. Yesterday we had a meeting with several of the COOs from our hospitals, my CEO and I. I did a position paper outlining four or five different ways in which you could structure relationships with docs, all the way from what we currently have in which everybody is independent, to a very controlled system where everybody is employed. There are a lot of different positions in between. I had to put it on one sheet of paper with six headings and a bunch of bullet points so that the nonphysician leaders could quickly grasp some of the pros and cons from the docs' points of view for each of the possibilities. You have to be able to put together concise little documents like that, but you also have to be able to create a Powerpoint® presentation where you are presenting your written word to the Board, Executive Committee, Credentials Committee, or your nursing staff. You have to able to be concise, use some graphics, and get your ideas across in the spoken or written word.

"Anyone who has seen the Health Care Advisory Board 2003 publication on this will quickly realize a good bit of it came from their approach, where they very nicely laid out all these possibilities. The difference is that each one there took up about five pages and what I had to do was distill it down to bullet points.

"You have to have a high amount of patience in this job. You can't let yourself get frustrated by all of the naysayers, because you have to remember the rule of ten. Ninety percent of your problems are created by ten percent of your players. We spend so much of our time dealing with that ten percent that sometimes we lose sight of the fact that a lot of people come here to work every day and do a damn good job. We don't celebrate our successes nearly as often as we should. I am going to try to do more of that."

Susan Freeman MD, MS, CPE, FACPE
Chief Medical Officer, Temple University Hospital, Philadelphia, PA

"One of the most effective communication skills I have used is presenting physicians with accurate data and helping them interpret the data so that they are actionable.

"A great deal of quality is dependent on maximizing physician efficiency and performance. You need to set expectations for physicians, measure their performance, and report it back to them in a meaningful manner. Example: An expectation would be when the emergency department calls, you need to return that call within 30 minutes. Someone needs to write down when you were called and when you called back. The expectation needs to be measurable.

"The role of the VPMA is to be a facilitator and resource to the medical staff leadership. One of the major mistakes VPMAs get into is that they take too much on their shoulders. They don't involve and get buy-in from some of the committees of the medical staff. That is a mistake, as I've learned through trial and error.

"It is the role of the VPMA to coordinate the activities, making sure that the medical staff has set expectations and that they are being followed, but when they are not being followed, it is the responsibility of the department chair to have a conversation with the physician. I talk with the department chairs.

"Lead by example. If you are practicing, you need to practice the way you want everyone else to practice. You make sure your patients are not sitting in the waiting room for hours. You can't always lead by example. When they don't see it, you measure it and communicate it.

"I have dealt with disruptive physicians in every job that I have had. In St Paul I was the one who confronted them. In Connecticut I had strong department chairs and they did it or we did it together.

"Good clear honest information that doesn't have spin is always the way that I've approached things. Example: We had some specialists in ob-gyn oncology. They were unhappy with their salaries and the kind of referrals they were getting. They went across town and were in negotiations with our competition, and they used that against us. We would do everything we could to keep them. But instead of communicating to the rest of the medical staff that they went across town and were negotiating with the competition, they were told we were delaying negotiations with them because of some things going on in the organization. We didn't exactly lie but we spun the information. I think it works much better if you don't do that, because the medical community is small and there are a lot of rumors. People really do talk to each other, people are married to each other, and the truth gets out eventually. Then you look like an idiot because you put spin on something that didn't really need to have spin on it."

Alan S. Kaplan MD, MMM, CPE, FACPE
Vice President, Chief Medical Officer & Operations, Edward Health Services Corporation
Naperville, IL

"I listen to people, I try to understand their point of view. I repeat back to them what they have told me. I consider all sides. I'm never afraid to make a hard decision, but if I do so, I go to that person, say I'm going to make a decision you don't like, here is what it is but this is why I am making it. I'm fair to my enemies and I don't favor my friends. Over time I believe that builds a lot of trust.

"If there is a crisis I don't get excited. I don't immediately blame anybody for anything. I always believe there are two sides to a story.

"There is an orthopedist on staff who is extremely disruptive. He is annoying. His response to the emergency department is poor. He is someone I would love to go away. There was conflict with him and a radiology technician. Everyone was ready to throw the book at this guy. He had a history. I sat down with him and heard the whole story. I realized there was a huge process problem in the file room that created frustration for this doctor every single day.

"Physicians would come in without telling the tech and take x-rays out and walk off with them. The surgeon comes in, can't find the x-ray, the tech doesn't know where it is because later we find out the radiologist came in and took it without checking it out. The surgeon is frustrated because it is taking up his day, he is late for the OR, and he starts yelling at the tech.

"Although I addressed his behavior, I also felt he had good reason to be upset. I downgraded the level of the offense. He acted out but it was instigated by a bad process. Then I worked hard to improve that process.

"When I took on more administrative duties, I had no job description. My responsibilities were working on the contracts with anesthesiology, pathology, and radiology, being a medical staff liaison—whatever that meant—and my usual medical director job.

[pushed him for an example of what liaison between administration and physicians means].
"All the trauma surgeons decided they were going to walk off trauma call. My CEO immediately goes to the threatening mode. I asked her not to do that. Let me talk to everyone first and understand where they are coming from, talk about the dynamics and see what we can do. She gave me some time.

"They were busy in their private practices and found trauma call a huge burden. They didn't feel it covered their expenses. They were getting $500 a night. They didn't want to do it anymore, but I knew that the general surgery call in my environment was very lucrative for them because they had a great payer mix. So I worked out a compromise. We upped the fees a little—$750—no more than market was at that time. I tied general surgery call to trauma call. General surgery call and trauma call by law have to be on different nights. I said to them, 'I won't let you take one unless you take both.'

"At first they didn't like it, but I knew they would come around because what that meant was if they dominated the trauma call, they would also dominate the surgery call, because new people and competitors wouldn't be able to get on the call schedule. They liked that. I didn't have to point that out. I knew they would get it.

"And then I made them understand how much I valued them. I would tell them all in a meeting in public in front of other people, individually, and in small groups. These guys are the soldiers. They really take care of the patients in the emergency department. We really need and appreciate them. I think between building that relationship of appreciation, giving them some more money and tying the schedule to a way that they could see it was to their advantage is what worked. It was 8 years ago, and we have never had a problem."

Now that you have read what communication skills physician executives find helpful in their jobs, I am going to discuss those skills in more depth.

Listening

Milo Frank says he asked a group of people how long they could pay attention to what someone was saying without letting their minds wander off to sex, money, or the other good things in life. He got "answers of anywhere from four hours to four seconds."[1] Listening takes enormous energy and discipline.

If you decide you are willing to expend the energy to listen, here are some techniques that will help you listen so people will want to give you important information and value you as a person who helps them solve problems:

- **Be quiet.** You cannot be listening if you are talking or if you are thinking hard about what you are going to say next. If you get very anxious about not knowing what to say when the person finishes, try putting all your energy into listening and then tell him or her, "I need to think about this. Can I get back with you in a while to talk more?"

  Roger Ailes, who coached the first President Bush during his presidential campaign, suggests that you should listen carefully before all interactions, particularly ones where you are scheduled to make a presentation. "When you enter a communication situation, don't immediately stand up and start projecting your voice and throwing out your opinions. Stop for a second, absorb what's going on. What's the mood of the room, the crowd—are they down, up, happy, expectant? Read what people are feeding back to you. Are they skeptical or eager?"[2] The only way to find this out is to be quiet and listen.

- **Use your body to let the person know you are there.** Look at him or her. Don't let your eyes wander all over the room. Sit attentively but not tensely, not slouching or lying down. On the sofa watching TV or reading the paper are not good positions for listening. Neither is opening your mail in your office while someone tries to tell you something. You may think you can do both, but the talker does not think you are listening and will be irritated.

- **Give an occasional "uh huh" or nod** to let the person know you are following his or her train of thought. If you are not, ask a question before you let the person go on too long and you are really lost.

- **Ask nonjudgmental questions.** "Can you say a little more? I'm not sure I understand. Will you try me again? What do you think that you'll do next?" Don't ask, "Why on earth did you do that?" There is absolutely no decent answer to that question, and the person doing the asking is implying, "You are an idiot!" You may be right, but if you want communication to continue, you will have to discipline yourself not to say everything you think.

  Good listening requires asking timely questions that help the person along with the story. "Think of the people you know whom you consider to be true leaders. When you are with them, they invariably ask questions. They are interested in you and your ideas. They are also interested in improving their listening skills."[3]

- **Restate some of what the person has said** to demonstrate that you understand. For example, "You think the nurses on the floor resent the patient coordinators because they don't do shift work anymore?" This is not necessary in every situation. Sometimes questions that ask for more information let the person know you are with them.

- **Make a guess about a feeling** you think the person is having if it seems appropriate. "I can see why that would make you sad." They may reply, "I'm not sad, I'm angry." It doesn't matter if you are wrong. They will correct you, and you have gotten to a deeper level of communication when you find out how someone feels about a subject. They will feel a sense of relief and sometimes release when they identify the feeling.

  If someone describes an automobile accident to you, your reply of "That must have been frightening" lets them know you may have felt that too. Often, we feel alone when we have negative feelings, as if no one else has felt them. There is great comfort in knowing someone else has lived through them.

Listening becomes even tougher in heated emotional situations when people are angry. Sometimes people come to your office obviously upset. If you are feeling strong and collected, it is helpful if you can let the emotional person vent for a few moments. You might then respond, "I can see that you are angry, and I'm not surprised. What can I do to help?" If you are not up to being in the presence of so much negative energy, you might say, "I'll be glad to talk about this when you are calmer."

Don't do the following activities until you have spent a significant time listening:

- Don't give advice.

- Don't pass judgment.

- Don't tell your own experience.

As a physician executive, you are paid to give advice and pass judgment, but it's a matter of timing. We tend to want to do these three behaviors quickly. Save them for last, after you have let the person talk for a while.

Talking One on One

Robert Jamplis, MD, former President and Chief Executive Officer of the Palo Alto Medical Foundation, Palo Alto, California, described a time when he wanted to convince his group of physicians to do something that would cost them a lot of money, but would benefit the organization in the long term. "We individually went out and talked to every single partner. It took us six months, with dinners and everything else. We had 130 partners. We just pounded this in, and we finally got a unanimous vote."[4]

When you are in a one-on-one conversation:

- Use the right amount of energy.

Pronounce your words clearly. Also, do not use a voice that is too loud. Listeners will try to get away from you if you do. Don't mumble or slur your words. Use whatever energy it takes to get your words across to the other person. The listener should not have to struggle to hear you or understand you.

- Avoid arrogance.

"[A]rrogance combined with ego is a barrier to managerial effectiveness....[O]ne physician was quoted as saying: 'I am a doctor of medicine and obviously my field is more difficult and more important than management. I know that my field is more important because it requires years of study to become qualified; one can become a manager by simple organization appointment and without special education. Therefore, not just anyone can practice in my field but anyone can indeed practice management. Management is a lesser function than my own, so if I can successfully practice my own specialty, I must readily be able to manage—and manage better than most managers. I thus transfer my level of expertise to any field that is of lesser difficulty than my own specialty.' Thus, the conviction of some physicians that medicine is superior to management is often coupled with the assertion that it is easy to transfer one's medical expertise and experience to administration and human resources management. Of all the personal factors mentioned that hinder one's management career, this is perhaps the most 'deadly' flaw."[5]

Your word choice, your tone of voice, the position of your head and eyes can all convey arrogance. If you are thinking how much smarter and better you are than the person you are talking to, there is a good chance that message will come through, even if your words are satisfactory. If you find yourself thinking in this way, try changing to this thought, "What will it cost me if I alienate this person?"

- Let the other person also talk.

Don't talk longer than a couple of minutes without letting the other person talk. An important part of speaking effectively is not speaking too much. "If most of the time you talk more than you listen, you're probably failing in your communication and probably boring people, too."[6]

Taking turns was a valuable thing to learn in preschool, and we never outgrow the need to do it. I've had people say, "Why should I give you a turn, if you can't fight to say what you want to say." Remember that Extroverts talk and then figure out what they think; Introverts figure out what they think and then talk. Introverts have valuable information if you give them a chance to say it. Seldom will they fight for air time, but they won't necessarily go along with decisions if they have had no input.

Extroverts sometimes talk too much. If you go on and on when you talk, people dread being around you. When they have to come to your office for a business conversation, they plan ways to get out before they ever come in. Jacquelyn Wonder, in *The Flexibility Factor*, describes a cure for a client who talked too much in meetings. He drew on paper an imaginary tongue depressor divided into four parts. He could speak four times in a meeting and then no more. He had a hard time controlling himself at first, but he finally accomplished his goal. Eventually, he didn't need the image of the tongue depressor on paper but carried it in his mind. Six months later, he said, "This is one of the most valuable changes I've ever made. I've found that I get so much more out of a meeting by listening to others. I'd always felt responsible for rushing in and filling gaps in conversation and responding to a lecturer. Now I don't feel the tension I used to when there was a moment of silence. I'm more apt to see the big picture than before, and I recall the meeting as a whole, rather than just bits and pieces."[7]

I have also recommended to people that they squeeze one hand with the other to remind them of a change they want to make. The mild pain is a signal to the brain not to keep talking.

Suppose you don't speak up enough. Before you go into a meeting or a conversation, write out what you might say on a particular issue. You will not read it, but if you have focused your thoughts beforehand, you are more willing to risk your ideas. Then set a goal to speak at least twice during the session. Put a check on the notes in front of you each time you speak. If you have trouble speaking up on an unexpected topic that is being discussed, pretend to take notes about what others are saying, but really write down what you'd like to say. Once you see what you've written and see that it makes good sense, you will be more willing to say it to the group.

- Be concise.

Suppose you want to tell someone something he or she does not want to hear. You have a list of 18 things they have done wrong. Don't tell them all of them. Pick two or three.

Go in and say, "I am hearing complaints from the people in the accounting department. Do you want to hear about them?" Then tell two or three things—not 18. Prioritize them. You don't say, "Everyone is mad at you because you don't treat them with respect." Instead be specific and say, "When Jim came to talk to you about the budget, he said you interrupted him after two sentences and said, "You are crazy if you think I'm going to give you that much money."

Body Language

What causes someone to understand you and respond well to you? Research suggests that:

— 7 percent of understanding depends on the words you use.

— 38 percent depends on your tone of voice.

— 55 percent depends on your nonverbal body language.

"The reality is that few people accept responsibility for anything more than their words. They have never learned that a harsh tone can deny the gentlest of words."[8] Inappropriate body language can negate your message. "I'm not angry" said loudly while you're pounding on a table changes the meaning of the message.

Don't point constantly when you talk or make any strange gesture repeatedly. Look at yourself on videotape to see if you have any odd mannerisms or make any unpleasant sounds. It is amazing how unaware we can be. I've seen people scratch places repeatedly that should only be touched in private. I've heard people say "uhm" so much that I began to count them.

What constitutes a good voice and good body language?

Voice

- "A positive voice is: cheerful, satisfied, concerned, warm," confident.

- "A negative voice is: sarcastic, scared, depressed, clipped, tense, too loud or soft.

Face and Body

- "Positive face has: smile, occasional head nod, and eye contact.

- "Negative face has: frown, smirk, boring glare," wandering eyes.

- "Positive body language is: relaxed, leaning forward some, open arms.

- "Negative body language is: pointing, wandering eyes, picking at body."[9]

Tone of voice and body language are important when you have to fire someone. When someone has to be let go, you need to get out of the frame of mind that views it as a depressing, devastating event. You need to rise above the despair and say, in a calm, confident tone of voice, "You are a good person who has worked hard, but your strengths are not matching what we need to have done in this position. We failed to pick this up in the interview. Your strengths as a writer and editor are valuable and you need to find a place where those are called upon. We will help you in the future, give you good recommendations. We will give you this much severance."

Presentations

Regularly surveys report that some people fear public speaking more than death. But for those willing to do it, there is great satisfaction in having an audience respond well to a talk you've given. It also makes money for your organization. When people see a physician or a physician executive make an impressive speech in the community, they often will go to that person's group for medical care.

The first step in speech preparation is to think about the people who will be listening to you. When you make a talk, you are selling yourself to your audience. In order to sell anything, you have to find out what people want. To do that, you must analyze your audience: Are its members male, female, young, old, a mixture? What's their cultural background? Will they understand your technical terms? If not, define them in a pleasant, noncondescending voice.

Pay attention to the language you use. Avoid unnecessary words and do not use overly long sentences. Generally, one idea per sentence is good. Figures of speech add color and excitement. ("Working in an emergency department is like walking through a mine field—one trauma exploding through the door after another." Or, "My life is like a roller coaster—up one minute and down the next.")

Unless you are very comfortable making speeches, write out exactly what you are going to say. Write it in a conversational style—not like an academic paper. Do not read the speech. Memorize it or learn it well enough that you do not say "um" while you are thinking of the next thing to say. Writing out the full speech reduces the "ums" of thinking time. When you know the speech well, your mind is freed of anxiety, and you will be able to add interesting examples to prove your points as you watch the reactions of the audience.

When you deliver the speech, stand erect with feet firmly on the floor. Don't lean on the flipchart stand or sit on a table. Look like you have the strength to be up there and entertain them. Use some gestures but not too many. Nothing is more distracting than watching someone who has just taken a course on public speaking and has added enough gestures to their talk to look like an ensign giving signals on a ship. Make direct eye contact with someone in each third of the room, slowly rotating your attention but in a random fashion. If you have the courage to look directly at a few people, the audience thinks you are confident.

Learn the beginning of the speech particularly well. That is when you are the most nervous and don't think as well. Look happy, confident, as if you can help them solve a problem. If you don't feel that way, pretend that you do. The old saying, "Fake it till you make it," really works. Shakespeare said, "Assume a virtue if you have it not." If you pretend you are cheerful and self-assured, you will soon begin to feel it. The reverse is not true. Sitting around waiting to feel great before a speech doesn't usually happen. Everyone is nervous. They just go ahead anyway. They learn to channel the nervousness into an energetic delivery.

Wear professional clothes. A dark blue or gray suit with light shirt, striped, paisley, or club tie is good for men. Women should wear a suit or tailored dress without low cut necklines or skirts too short.

After you've written the speech and considered these do's and don'ts—PRACTICE. The more you sweat ahead of time, the less you sweat on stage. Practice in front of a mirror; in front of a friend who will give you honest feedback; or, best of all, in front of a video camera. Record yourself, watch it, and record again until you are pleased with your performance.

Pulling Teams Together—Meetings

No matter what the topic of the meeting you are having, people are worrying about three things according to William Shultz—inclusion, control, and affection. Inclusion deals with issues of acceptance. Will I be liked? How can I get to know these people? Will I let them know me? Control deals with the issue of power. Will I be listened to? Will I be able to get others to do some of what I want them to? What will I have to do to be a part of this group? Affection concerns how much group members care for each other. Do I care about others in this group, and am I willing to show it? Do they care about me, and will they show it?[10]

As the leader, how do you deal with these issues?

Inclusion

Be sure each person speaks during the meeting—the sooner the better. If they speak at the beginning of the meeting, they will usually feel included and pay closer attention. You can have people first write and then tell what they had to go through to get to the meeting or what task they left to come to the meeting. If it's a group of people who do not know each other, have them introduce themselves and then tell something about themselves.

Control

If it is a small group, you need ideas from everyone at the meeting. Otherwise there was no reason to call them together. You will always have some Extroverts and some Introverts. Extroverts want to talk immediately and at length. Introverts want to have time to think before they speak. Because Extroverts want to jump on a topic after you have barely finished laying it out and talk a lot as they figure out what they really think about a topic by sorting out the ideas aloud, you, as the leader, must exert some control over the meeting and provide an opportunity for each type to contribute valuable ideas. If you have everyone write on a topic for the first three minutes after it is brought up, the Introverts have the quiet time needed to collect their thoughts. The Extroverts have been forced to wait a few minutes, and then you can feel free to call on everyone to contribute his or her thoughts.

Do not let talkers dominate the meeting. If someone attacks someone, try to move in and stop it. You might say, "I don't think this criticism is constructive. Do you have a suggestion of a change we can make?"

Affection

Showing affection may or may not be appropriate for your group. Members of some groups hug each other. In other groups, affection is shown by allowing talk about some personal concerns in addition to tending to business. The group may meet for coffee. If group members sense that others care about them, they are more productive, more willing to come to the meetings.

Long before a meeting begins, envision likely questions and problems so you can deal with them. Use the process recommended in the book, *The Inner Game of Tennis*. Just as you would visualize the correct tennis shot, "Visualize your meeting in advance. Picture the perfect attitude of the group, the perfect location, the perfect proposal, the perfect discussion, the perfect argument. Visualize the perfect response to the difficult participant. Visualize the perfect meeting and then make the necessary preparations to make that vision a reality."[11]

Try saying and picturing in your mind, "I will run a productive meeting where all the agenda topics are discussed and decided upon. People will cooperate." If you keep seeing it happen, it has a much better chance of happening than if you constantly ruminate about how Dr. Adams is going to negatively filibuster any changes that are suggested. Go talk to Dr. Adams ahead of time and try to win him over to your side, even if it requires giving him something he wants in order to get something you want.

If you know you cannot win over a dissenter, consider changing your plans. "If I have something on the agenda that is really important to me, I always know where the votes are before I go into that meeting,' says lawyer and investment banker Peter Kelly. By doing this, you can make a judgment to move ahead on your item, to do a little extra homework, or to take it off the agenda if your count shows you can't win."[12]

Conflict-Confrontation-Anger

Knowing who to confront, when to confront, what to say, and how to say it is no simple task. Most people dread it. Don't expect that you won't. Even if you polish your technique, you still may procrastinate and have butterflies in your stomach when it comes time to do it. Some people report such extreme physical reactions as diarrhea, nausea, palpitating heart, and sweaty palms.

However, I have met a few physicians who truly seem to crave power, thrive on angry confrontation, and feel the joy of the kill when humiliating others with emotional outbursts. I suspect some of them went into medicine with a desire for power that would allow them to behave badly. Before the health care scene dramatically began to change in the late '80s and '90s, they could get by with such behavior for an entire career. With increased competition, some organizations are saying, "You simply cannot behave that way anymore. If you do, you will lose your job." "Problem employees who are not dealt with fairly and promptly will produce avoidable problems, demonstrate to others that poor behavior is okay, and subvert your management authority."[13]

The word confrontation usually has a negative connotation for most people. Try to switch your thinking to, "It is important that I learn to ask for what I want. Others should not be forced to read my mind."

Neither an angry voice nor a weak voice is effective in confrontation. Some people propel themselves into a confrontation with the use of anger. They usually meet with open rebellion or subversive behavior that undermines what they are trying to get accomplished. They tell people what to do, but somehow the projects are sabotaged. An anesthesiologist screams, "How many times have I told you this is not the proper set up for someone with cardiac problems?" The technicians get even with the physician by continuing to not set up properly and watching him explode.

Others ask for what they want with such a weak tone of voice and weak words that people do not take them seriously. "Would you mind not coming late for your shift?" A better way to say it is, "I have to stay late when you don't show up on time for your shift. I need to pick up my children. Please be on time."

Find an appropriate place for the confrontation. The hall will not do. "When the opportunity arises to compliment individuals for success and, even more important, for team success, a manager must do it well and let others in the organizations know about it. When it is necessary to correct, counsel, or admonish someone for any reason, it must be in private."[13]

Use a calm, firm voice with eye contact. Don't repeat your message in the beginning. Sometimes we deliver the message and then, either because we are nervous or we think the listener is ignoring us, we say it again and again. If you ramble on and repeat yourself, people discount you and tune you out. Say your major points and then wait for a reaction. It is not your job to try to make the other person comfortable by filling the air space with words. Also, you cannot afford the leisure of making yourself comfortable with constant chatter. Let there be silence or let the person blow up and just watch calmly. If the person explodes, let them blow. Do not become overly defensive. Stick to your major points.

If you are confronting someone about unacceptable behavior and you are met with much resistance and denial, you may have to repeat the message. Example: "Throwing instruments is unacceptable behavior in our organization." Becoming a broken record and repeating the message after you've listened to much denial is very different from saying the same message two or three different ways when you are beginning the conversation. The former shows firm conviction. The latter indicates nervousness and unsureness.

Discuss no more than three concerns in a confrontation—one is better. If you bring up too many issues you weaken your position. You cannot solve 20 years of irritation in one encounter. Don't bring up what happened in 1995. The more you confront things as they come up, the less you'll need to deal with all past hurts on the few occasions when you get the courage to say something.

You have a right to ask for what you want. You may not always get it, but, in this country, you can ask for it.

You do not have a right to yell for what you want and humiliate others with sarcasm in the process. Some of you may be thinking, "Oh, yes I do." If so, I encourage you to sit down and think about your relationships. Are the people who work with and for you cooperative? Are your patients leaving? Do your family members look forward to your coming home at night?

You also have a right to change how you behave in the relationship if you do not get what you want. For example, if family members will not pick up their own clothes after you have repeatedly asked them to, you can stop washing them. If physicians will not keep their charts up to date, you can intercept them as they enter the hospital to have charts completed.

Try not to use the big emotions of anger and tears in a confrontation. Some people use anger to try to get what they want; others use tears. Neither is very effective. People feel threatened, frightened, or repulsed by a show of uncontrolled emotion. However, if these emotions occur in others, try to remain calm and strong and not let them throw you off balance.

If you need to have an important confrontation or you have had an interaction that didn't go well, here's a process that may help you confront the person.

- Write out what you want to say or wish you had said and write how angry you are. Let all your emotions spill onto the page. Cuss them. Hold nothing back, but don't show this to anyone.

- Go for a 30-minute walk.

- Write again what you want to say. This time you'll find you don't need to say as many of the nasty things. Come up with three major points you want to make when you actually talk to the person.

  1. Explain your view of the situation.

     "I've gotten numerous complaints that you are yelling at co-workers and at times are even rude to patients. I've talked to you about this twice in the past six months. You do better for several weeks and then begin the same old behavior."

  2. Tell what you want.

     "This has to stop. I want you to get help to try to alleviate your anger and learn some better ways to communicate."

  3. Say what will happen if you do not get it.

     "If this continues, you will lose your job."

You may not always say the third point, but it is important for you to know. It gives you a sense of power, and people can detect it when you have it. When my children were small, and I was feeling exhausted, they would misbehave, because they sensed and probably feared weakness in me. Sometimes, I went across the street to complain to a neighbor who would help me come up with a plan. I'd walk back in the house with a strong countenance and a game plan. The children would take one look, see that the power was back, and shape up. Many times, I never had to do a thing. They seemed to be able to sniff the power in the air. The same is true for adults. If you look meek or unnecessarily mean, you probably will get noncooperation or rebellion. Find that middle ground that is firm but reasonable.

As a back-up plan, you need to know ahead of time what you are going to do if the person will not meet you half way on at least some of the points. You may not use this bargaining chip, but you need to have it in your mental pocket. People can sense power and they can sense weakness. If you have the back-up plan, the room is filled with power.

If you have no bargaining chip, don't keep trying to make the person change if you know he or she won't. Don't keep whining that you wish they would behave better. Every time you beg, you lose self-esteem and feel more humiliated.

In the '60s and '70s, much was written about the value of venting when you were angry. The advice was to really let the people know who have wronged you. I disagree. Few situations are improved with loud expressions of anger. Usually they just get hotter. Dr. Pierce Howard, in *The Owner's Manual for the Brain*, says, "The emotion of angry hostility places us in a double-bind: both holding it in and venting it are bad for the heart and the immune system. The secret to dealing with anger is to express it without getting angry. Get it out, deal with it, and get over it."[14]

Anger is a physical phenomenon as well as a mental one. You will feel it somewhere in your body—clinched fists, knots in your stomach, gritted teeth, tight neck, somewhere—because adrenaline is rushing through your system. You need to get it out of your body in a physical way, but there are many ways to do it besides screaming at the person who has angered you. Go for a run or a very fast walk. Play golf and pretend the ball is the offending person's head that you are slamming down the fairway. Write quickly without stopping, telling the person how rotten he or she is and what you want to do to him or her. (But don't let anyone see it.) You need to get the anger out of your system, but you don't want to dump it on the wrong person or even necessarily on the offending person.

There may be a few times when it is appropriate to get angry and let the person know it. Sometimes, people have to be matched with the same amount of force they are sending out. Not backing down on your position, looking mean, and raising your voice are essential to let the person know you can do it. I yelled only a few times when I was raising teenagers, and they speak of it still. They had to know I was capable of that much force. But you need to be careful not to do that often. Don't confront every issue just because you learn how to do it. Pretend you have five confrontation bullets, and they need to last you five years. Don't use them up too quickly or use them on small problems. Save them for big problems. Spilling juice on the kitchen floor is not a big problem; driving under the influence of alcohol is.

If you feel the occasion warrants an outburst and you simply must do it, do it once. If you don't get the results you want, next time confront in a calm, calculated manner with a plan for what you are going to do if the person does not meet your demands. Continuing to hysterically blow your top weakens your position, even though you may experience a temporary sense of power and a release of tension.

If you need courage to confront, try a technique employed by American Indians. They used "'power chants' as centering devices to keep their hearts open and their minds clear at times of great danger. Each Indian brave repeated a particular affirmation of courage over and over until it became so familiar it was second nature to him. That way, in a crisis he wouldn't have to think about it or try to remember the words of the chant. They would be right there at the tip of his tongue."[15]

If you need to calm down and not lose your temper, "call for a time out ('I'm too upset to talk about this anymore—I'd like to take a break and talk some more later.')."[16] Learning a relaxation technique can also help you gain control. Anger and relaxation cannot exist in the body at the same time. One rules out the other. After you have practiced the relaxation technique for at least three weeks, one or two deep breaths can help you control your reactions.

Take whichever approach will help you, but don't avoid the interaction too long. We are all different, and we must let each other know our needs in a calm, firm, effective manner.

Writing

Physician executives are called upon to write—emails, memos, letters, reports, or articles. In many places email has replaced the use of memos. Keep emails as short as possible. With hundreds in people's inboxes, no one wants to scroll down to see more words on the screen. Memos stay inside the office and often travel up and down the hierarchical structure. Letters go outside the office and have to be dressed up a little better than memos. Reports often go to superiors. If you want any of them to be read by busy people, they must be short and sweet. The traditional academic style of writing will serve you well for clinical articles, but if you write for management journals, your style needs to be clear and less burdened with academic jargon.

Most of us get the necessary emails, memos and letters written, even though we would rather do something else. But many people have said to me that they want to write an article or a book but just can't seem to get themselves to do it. Writing for publication lets people know who you are and what you think. It enhances your career, because people will consider you for specific jobs. It's a good networking technique, because it puts your name before people as an expert. I'll talk first about how to stop dreading the writing process so much, no matter what you need to write, and then about how to edit so you have a document you are proud of.

Frequently, when people have a writing project to do, they carry around with them a sense of gloom—I should do it, but I don't want to. They sharpen pencils, go to the bathroom, get another cup of coffee, clean out desk drawers that have been messy for months, go talk to someone at the water cooler—all tasks that seem urgent, certainly more important than putting the first word on the page.

If you want to stop procrastinating on writing projects, pick up a pen and write 10 minutes a day in a journal. A journal is whatever kind of paper you like. I'll describe it in more detail in Chapter 12.

Writing should be a two-part process—generating ideas and editing those ideas. Never do both at the same time.

Generating Ideas

If you are writing along and can't decide which of two words to use in a sentence, write both of them down and keep going. "It's an unnecessary burden to try to think of words and also worry at the same time whether they are the right words."[17] If you stop to decide, the left hemisphere of your brain, which passes judgment on the quality of your work, wakes up and begins the censoring process. You have spent a fair amount of time lulling it into a rest mode by writing quickly without stopping. If you let it begin to work while you are brainstorming using the right hemisphere, the right side may stop sending ideas. All instructions for brainstorming in meetings say you must not judge anyone's ideas during the process of thinking of all the ideas you can come up with. The same is true when you are alone and brainstorming with pen and paper.

When you are having a difficult time making yourself write, start writing whether you feel like it or not. You may think you have no ideas at all on a subject, but, as Peter Elbow says about his own writing "you are making a serious error....You are mistaking lousy, stupid, second-rate, wrong, childish, foolish, worthless ideas for no ideas at all."[18] If you keep doing 10-minute writing exercises you will eventually find ideas you like. If you just sit, chew your pencil, wait for the ideas to come, they may never come at all. People use the term writer's block for this condition. It probably should be called writer's procrastination or writer's perfection. We all want great ideas to come on the first attempt, because it feels wonderful to be that brilliant. Occasionally, people do write great words on the first try, but it is rare. Also, we don't want to have to do the dreaded writing process a second time. When you decide to freewrite, all the pressure is off. You know it doesn't have to be good, so you just get started easier. People usually become hooked on this process the first time they experience writing something wonderful in the midst of lots of grumbling words complaining about the writing process.

It's not hard to write a journal entry if you give yourself permission for it to be lousy. If you will begin to pay your dues to the writing gods by writing anything that comes to mind everyday for a week, I assure you some good ideas will surprise you and turn up on the page in front of you almost as if you were taking dictation from some other-worldly source. "[A] person's best writing is often mixed up together with his worst. It all feels lousy to him as he's writing, but if he will let himself write it and come back later, he will find some parts of it are excellent. It's as though one's best words come wrapped in one's worst."[19] This is why you need to freewrite and put lots of words on paper—so you can find the good ones in the midst of much garbage.

You must put down enough words, whether good or bad, to get the writing process started. You exercise your hand and brain the same way an athlete trains for his or her sport. I find I rarely can skip the training process. If I have not been writing regularly in my journal, and I have a writing project due, it takes 5-10 days of 10-minute writing sessions to get back to producing sentences I like.

Editing

Once you have generated enough ideas and have written a draft of the paper, it is time to put on the hat of an editor and clean up the copy. "Every word omitted keeps another reader with you."[20] Editing is not as difficult if you have plenty of words to work with. You can pick the good and throw away the bad without worrying that there won't be enough left. Also, if you have generated the draft with a freewriting, devil-may-care attitude, you have not sacrificed so much to write the words, and you are more willing to cut.

"Editing means figuring out what you really mean to say, getting it clear in your head, getting it unified, getting it into an organized structure, and then getting it into the best words and throwing away the rest. It is crucial, but it is only the last step" in the writing process."[21] I've found if I read a draft the first thing in the morning for about five days, I'll edit more easily. Somehow I see things in the morning that I'll let slip later in the day.

Instead of trying to worry about all the rules of usage and grammar; I've picked a few that deal with how to be concise.

- **Avoid needless repetition.** It is fine to use the same word over and over when you are generating thoughts. As a matter of fact, the subconscious seems to send us messages that way. Often, a first draft of a paper will have a word repeated 5 to 10 times. When you are editing, circle all the repeated words and try to eliminate most of them, unless you are repeating the word to emphasize its importance or changing the word would confuse the reader. Examples:

  Too much repetition: Businesses want to decorate their offices with low-maintenance plants. Philodendrons and scheffleras are some low-maintenance plants. These plants are inexpensive.

  Improved: Businesses want to decorate their offices with inexpensive, low-maintenance plants, such as philodendrons and scheffleras.

- **Avoid redundancy.** Being redundant means that you write the same idea a second time, but use different words. End result, final conclusion, personal opinion, and unexpected surprise are examples of redundancy. Instead of the extra words used in a redundant phrase, cut to the simplest word. Clarity is better than stuffy sophistication. Examples:

advance reservations	reservations
basic necessities	needs
cease and desist	stop
each and every	all
first and foremost	first

- **Always use fewer words** rather than more words to express an idea. Examples:

in the event that	if
in order to	to
in the amount of	for
in view of the fact that	because

- **Use precise words** that convey a specific visual image rather than vague words. Examples:

nice house	brick house
pickup	Dodge wide cab
car	Jaguar

- **Choose strong verbs** rather than verbs hidden in many words. Examples:

make application to	apply
give assistance	help
make a decision	decide

- **Avoid jargon.** Jargon, in its broadest definition, is any language that is hard to understand. Sometimes it acts as a shield for those who don't have much to say. It can be specialized vocabulary that a particular group of people understand. Teenagers find a different set of words every two or three years that, they hope, will confuse their parents. Accountants, chemists, bankers, doctors, and others have their special terms that must be defined when they are working with the general public.

  Often jargon is phony, inflated, and uselessly complex language. A client told me once, "If I speak and write so others understand me, they will steal my job." I think jargon hurts you more than it might help you keep your job. People get angry if you use difficult words without explaining their meaning. They delete your email or put your memos in the trash and do not do what you have asked them to do.

  The passage below from Moby Dick has lost its clarity and beauty through the addition of jargon.[22]

  The Original

  "Call me Ishmael. Some years ago—never mind how long precisely—having little or no money in my purse and nothing in particular to interest me on shore, I thought I would sail about a little and see the water part of the world."

  Jargon Added

  "You may identify me by the nomenclature of Ishmael. At a point in time several years previous to the current temporal zone—the precise number of which is extraneous information—devoid of sufficient monetary resources and lacking physical and/or psychical stimuli within the confines of my sphere of activity on land, I initiated several thought processes and concluded that I would commandeer a vessel of navigation with which to explore the aquatic component of this planet."

- **Eliminate overused words.** Overworked expressions make a reader switch from paying attention to your message to being irritated that you are saying the same old thing. "The bottom line," "the whole nine yards," and "I need your input" are phrases that need a few years' rest.

  If you can finish the following statements, they have probably been overused. Try filling in the blanks.[23]

  It has come to our…

  Please call at your earliest…

  We regret to…

  If you have additional questions, feel…

  Enclosed…

- **Use the active voice** unless you have a specific reason not to. In the active voice, the subject performs the action of the verb and appears in the first part of the sentence.

Example: The recruiting staff made three visits.

Using the passive voice reverses the order of the nouns in the sentence and adds a form of "to be" (is, am, are, was, were, be, being, been) to the verb.

Example: Three visits were made by the recruiting staff.

Using the passive voice adds unnecessary words to a sentence and robs the verb of its straightforward power. There are times when the passive voice is appropriate. Perhaps you don't want to tell who is doing what. Example: "Valuable resources are being wasted."24 However, most of us use it too often and weaken our messages. Use the active voice as much as possible.

Examples:

An appointment can be made for you.	Passive voice
I can make an appointment for you.	Active voice
The new design was spoken about by Dr. Johnson.	Passive voice
Dr. Johnson spoke about the new design.	Active voice

A Short Grammar Lesson

I am going to discuss one grammar mistake that I hear often. Fewer and fewer people use pronouns correctly. As an English teacher, I used to become so irritated when I heard some sentences that I lost the content. But then I began to remind myself of my math weaknesses. Life goes on if I cannot figure percentages quickly or do math word problems.

However, I am going to make a stab at explaining the correct usage of personal pronoun in the subject and object slot of a sentence. These two sentences are wrong.

1. *Me and John went to the store.*
   Subject slot

2. *She gave the report to Mary and I.*
   Object slot

Here are the forms of the personal pronoun when they go in the subject slot:

I	We
You	You
He, she, it	They

The grammatically correct version of sentence 1 is:

John and I went to the store. (Be polite and put the other person first in the sentence.)

Here are the forms of the personal pronouns when used in the object slot:

Me	Us
You	You
Him, her, it	Them

The correct version of sentence 2 is:

She gave the report to Mary and me.

(A way to test what works here is to take out the other person's name. We instinctively know to say, She gave the report to me rather than to I.

Use the object form of the personal pronouns after prepositions. Here's a list of prepositions that often have a pronoun used after them

About

Against

Beside

Between

By

For

From

In

Into

Of

On

Under

With

So the correct version of often-used prepositional phrases is:

The reports were divided between John and me. (Not between John and I)

The presentation evaluations were good for Mary and me. (Not for Mary and I)

Jane gave the new stationery to Sandra and me. (Not to Sandra and I)

You can always test the correct version by taking out the other person's name. You wouldn't say, "She gave the stationery to I." You know it doesn't sound right.

In the last part of this chapter I have become very picky, and some of you may think I sound like an old school marm. These suggestions are for the editing phase—the last part of the writing process.

When you are generating ideas, you need a carefree, relaxed feeling about your writing.

Whatever pops in your head goes down on the page. When you edit, you use a critical eye and cut everything away but the straightforward information. If I need to edit, sometimes I will go to my flower bed and pull weeds to get me in the proper frame of mind. Editing is an absolutely essential part of writing, because no one wants to read all the aimless rambling that a human brain is capable of producing, but do not cause that editing shift to happen in the early stages of producing ideas. Once you have a good quantity of words on the page, you'll enjoy arranging them in a pleasing way. But if you have a blank page in front of you and let yourself think like an editor, you'll probably experience the overriding fear that there are no words in you. You'll have plenty of words when you sit down to write if they don't have to be perfect when they are first born.

References

1. Frank, M. *How to Get Your Point Across in 30 Seconds—or Less.* New York, N.Y.: Simon and Schuster, 1986, p. 15.

2. Ailes, R., with Kraushar, J. *You Are The Message.* Homewood, Ill.: Dow Jones-Irwin, 1988, p. 39.

3. Bethel, S. *Making a Difference. 12 Qualities That Make You a Leader.* New York, N.Y.: Berkley Books, 1990, p.205.

4. Robert Jamplis, President and CEO, Palo Alto Medical Foundation, personal communication, Feb. 1995.

5. Peters, R. *When Physicians Fail as Managers.* Tampa, Fla.: American College of Physician Executives, 1994, p. 28.

6. Ailes, R., *op. cit.*, p. 52.

7. Wonder, J., and Donovan, P. *The Flexibility Factor.* New York, N.Y.: Ballantine Books, 1989, pp. 216-7.

8. Alexander, J. *Dare to Change.* New York, N.Y.: A Signet Book, New American Library, 1984, p. 138.

9. Swets, P. *The Art of Talking So That People Will Listen.* Englewood Cliffs, N.J.: Prentice-Hall. Inc., 1983, p. 59.

10. Turner, N. *Effective Leadership in Small Groups.* Valley Forge, Pa.: Judson Press, 1977, pp. 17-9.

11. Kieffer, G. *The Strategy of Meetings.* New York, N.Y.: Simon and Schuster, 1988, p. 157.

12. *Ibid.*, p. 156.

13. Harris, C. "Physicians in Managed Care: Middle Management." In *Physicians in Managed Care: A Career Guide.* Tampa, Fla.: American College of Physician Executives, 1994, p. 88.

14. Howard, P. *The Owner's Manual for the Brain.* Austin, Tex.: Leornian Press—A Bard and Stephen Book, 1994, p. 153.

15. Arapakis, M. *Softpower.* New York, N.Y.: Warner Books, 1990, p. 151.

16. *Ibid.*, p. 152.

17. Elbow, P. *Writing Without Teachers.* London, England: Oxford University Press, 1973, p. 5.

18. *Ibid.*, p. 62.

19. *Ibid.*, p. 69.

20. *Ibid.*, p. 41.

21. *Ibid.*, p. 38.

22. Kolin, P. *Successful Writing at Work*. Lexington, Mass.: D. C. Heath and Company, 1986. (Originally appeared in Brown Alumni Monthly, Feb. 1981.)

23. Brill, L. *Business Writing Quick and Easy, 2nd Edition*. New York, N.Y.: American Management Association, 1989, p. 83.

24. Fielden, J. "What Do You Mean You Don't Like My Style?" *Harvard Business Review* 60(3):128-36, May-June 1982.

Other Reading

Lucas, S. *The Art of Public Speaking*. New York, N.Y.: Random House, 1986.

Chapter Seven

Networking —
Getting to Know More People

One of the first and often the most difficult tasks for job seekers is to increase the size of their networks—the number of people they know. You need to get to know more people than you know now. Most people get a job because they know someone who knows someone that led to the position. People have to know who you are and what you can do in order to recommend you for a job. They need to see you tackling problems and working with people. I've known a few people who didn't have all the experience that the organization wished that they had, but someone knew them and thought they had the qualities it would take to do the job. In this time of lessened job security, networking should be an ongoing process, something you are always doing, so that when you need a new position, you have people you already know that you can contact.

"Networking, which in the broadest sense is the maintaining of active friendships with your professional colleagues, helps you to stay current with developments in health care across the country."[1]

Networking comes easily for some people, usually those who are naturally gregarious. They heartily greet everyone they encounter, ask them probing questions, talk about their accomplishments, and come away knowing the person's name and several memorable facts about them. Other people cringe at intruding on someone's private space, resist asking seemingly nosy questions, feel that boasting is offensive, and don't mind that they cannot remember the name of the person they just talked to. Even though it is difficult for some, networking is an essential part of the job search.

"Some people have said, 'I know everyone in my hospital, but I don't belong to any outside associations, and I don't go to lunch with people from other hospitals and other facilities. I just kind of like my own group.' The job search will be much more difficult if you don't have a broad network."[2]

Sometimes people have felt that they should not get jobs through connections—almost as if that was cheating. If they were good enough, they could get the job all by themselves. That's just not the way it usually happens, so you must face that you have to play the game because it's the only one in town. Another prevalent attitude is that networking is using people. If you return the favor or pass it on somehow, someday, it's not using; it's what we all need—help from each other.

"Physicians are not used to networking. They are used to talking to people that they were in medical school with, but they don't know how to take it to the next step—talking to that person in order to get a referral to a stranger that they don't know."[3]

Gary Cohn in the *Wall Street Journal* says that management consultants and executive recruiters recommend, "DON'T BE SHY: The best way for an executive to gain entry to a company is through a personal recommendation, so pull out all the stops to get the word around you're available. Executives seeking upper-level jobs should generally seek help from upper-level contacts." Cohn also claims that 70 percent of jobs are landed because of personal contacts, 15 percent from placement agencies, 10 percent from direct mailings, and 5 percent from published openings.[4]

Sometimes you can even "create a job for yourself by contacting the appropriate person, explaining how you can satisfy that unmet need, and making an offer to work for them as a project manager or a consultant."[5]

To network you must increase your visibility—make speeches, write articles, lead committees, become president of the medical staff. Make phone calls, attend meetings and talk to people while you are there, send letters, send thank you notes, call people again, read journals for advertised positions, contact search firms. It's more work than most people want to do, but few people get to skip it. Larry Tyler, CEO of the executive search firm Tyler and Company, says, "Networking is tough, but not working is tougher."[6]

Experts disagree on what is appropriate networking behavior. I am going to describe two opposing views and hope you will pick the one that seems most appropriate for the person you are talking to.

Anna Navarro, an experienced coach, says, "You should never ask for a job in a networking interview, either directly ('Do you have any openings?') or indirectly ('Have your heard of any openings?'). That puts the person with whom you're meeting on the spot, and it is inappropriate networking behavior." However, she says, you can use networking to get a frank opinion of your strengths and weaknesses, feedback on your resume.[7]

Larry Tyler has a different point of view. He says, "Don't be reluctant to call professionals you have not met and talk to them about opportunities for yourself. You will be surprised at the number of total strangers who will go out of their way to give you a job lead or a piece of advice."[8] He also describes exactly how to have the conversation:

"'Mr. Johnson, thank you for returning my call. As I told your secretary, I was referred to you by (fill in the blank). I am in the process of changing position and am seeking your (any of the following: advice, counsel, input, suggestions) as to opportunities that might exist for a person with my background and abilities'....[T]ell him briefly about yourself and the type of position that interests you....[D]o not ask Mr. Johnson if that type of position is open in his organization, because you want his referrals and advice first. How your conversation progresses will depend on how much time Mr. Johnson wants to spend and what kind of rapport you establish on the phone. You should get the names of several people Mr. Johnson thinks might either have an opening or who might be good network leads. Ask if it is all right if you tell the referral where I got their names."[9]

Once you have accepted the fact that you must network, exactly how do you go about it? Make phone calls and then follow up with e-mails or letters so people will have a written reminder of your conversation. If you want to move to the Southeast, contact your medical school alumni office and find out which of your classmates live there. Then call them. Take the time to inquire about their lives before you immediately say what you want. Then, "Jan and I have always wanted to move back to your part of the country when the children were grown. I've been a VPMA here in Kansas for the past five years. Do you know of any management opportunities in your area?" And so on. You have a right to politely ask for information. You do not have a right to be pushy. The world out there does not owe you a contact just because you have gotten up, or have always had, the nerve to ask for one.

Attend meetings where people are gathered who are doing what you want to do. Here are some choices: American College of Physician Executives (ACPE), American College of Healthcare Executives (ACHE), Medical Group Management Association (MGMA), American Medical Group Association (AMGA), American Hospital Association (AHA)

Keep up with people from your past. "Your former employees and coworkers, especially the hard-working and ambitious ones, are an excellent source of potential members for your network. Stay in touch with them after either they or you leave your organization."[10]

Networking can begin with friends and family, but it usually has to go beyond that. "Being referred to a stranger by someone we know is a preferred course since we get an introduction. It makes the discussions easier and we feel better about the process. Eventually, however, we will have to introduce ourselves to strangers without any prior contact."[11]

Networking is not just begging for a job when you need one, although it is letting people know you are looking. It's ongoing, keeping up with people, staying in relationships, talking to people at meetings, calling occasionally to see how they are doing, writing a note of thanks when appropriate. Networking is also being visible. Without being obnoxious, let people see what you can do. Dress well, speak well. Volunteer to speak on something. Do a good job; give people valuable information. They'll remember you and think of you for a job. "Write for professional journals to create awareness or expertise. Get e-mail addresses of people, follow forums in the field, and communicate your knowledge."[12]

People who find networking extremely difficult are sometimes more comfortable writing articles and giving speeches as a way to be visible to others. Also, "when you read a thought-provoking article in one of your professional journals, you should copy it and send it to people who might be interested in it."[13]

Even as they try diligently to increase their networks, some very bright people have trouble remembering names no matter what mnemonic games they try. One physician who had just learned a remembering trick said he met someone with the last name Dasher. He thought no problem—one of Santa's reindeer. He said that, over time, he called that man everything—Donner, Prancer, Vixen. Even if you have this problem, keep trying to remember. Be friendly, and maybe they will remember you. Whenever possible, write the name down and something about the person. Sometimes writing will imprint the name in your brain. Keep a file of the names, where you met, what they had on. Sometimes a bright color will stay with you as a reminder.

Before you go to a cocktail party or call someone on the phone, do your homework. Dale Carnegie described how thoroughly Theodore Roosevelt did his homework: "Whether his visitor was a cowboy or a Rough Rider, a New York politician or a diplomat, Roosevelt knew what to say....Whenever Roosevelt expected a visitor, he sat up late the night before, reading up on the subject in which he knew his guest was particularly interested. For Roosevelt knew, as all leaders know, that the royal road to a person's heart is to talk about the things he or she treasures most.[14]

If you are planning to go to a cocktail party at an ACPE meeting, be sure you have read at least the current issue of the *Physician Executive Journal* or ideally the past several issues so you have possible topics of conversation. You may want to talk specifically to the author of an article who may be there. Many physicians write for the journal.

Also read the *New England Journal of Medicine*, *Modern Healthcare*, and other health care management and medical publications for advertised openings. Look at on-line job listings. You may want to find someone from a particular organization at the meeting and ask them what it is like to work there.

Go through the list of attendees at a meeting when you arrive and see who is from an area where you would like to live and work. Find them at a session or cocktail party and talk to them about what they do. Don't just go up and tell them you are looking for a job. People are put off by that because they may not know of anything or they feel burdened by your request. "The worst strategy is to appear needy. If you are mentally carrying a begging bowl, you invite rejection....When meeting new people, your primary task is to project competence and confidence."[15] Get to know the person by asking questions and listening. Your turn to talk will come if you invest time in the relationship.

When you talk to people in a social setting, you are looking for ways to connect with them. Here are some possible areas where you might find something in common:
- College (schools)— You went to the same one or know someone who went there
- Location — You lived in the same place at one time or know someone in their town
- Hobbies
- Sports
- Service clubs
- Professional societies
- Health club
- Religion
- Nationality[16]

These are ice-breaker topics in the beginning of networking conversations. Whenever you find a connection, you feel closer to the person and have a better chance of remembering each other.

Also, before a social event, rehearse a two-sentence introduction, especially if making contacts is difficult for you. You should be able to tell who you are and what you do without hesitation, fumbling, or rambling. Example: "I'm Barbara Linney, Vice President of Career Development for the American College of Physician Executives. I work with physicians who are thinking about making changes in their careers or who want to polish their communication skills." Or a version that doesn't use the title or name of the organization: "I work for an organization that teaches management education to physicians who are moving into administrative positions."

"Networking is exchanging information, resources, and support in such a way that you build a relationship."[17] Without purpose, small talk becomes just pleasant schmoozing, chatting about the ball game, or commiserating about the weather. That may pass the time, but it's not networking.[18]

If you want information from someone in particular, try to find out something about the person ahead of time. Talk to someone else who knows him or her. Then you have a conversation opener. Example: "Jake mentioned that your organization was planning to open an office in Memphis. How soon do you think it will be before it is operational?"

When you meet people, ask them what they do, tell them what you do, and patiently let a friendship evolve. "[Y]ou should pose the most often asked question in the English language: 'What do you do for ABC?' It's not original, but it's 100 percent, red-white-and-blue normal and what people expect."[19] "People generally like to talk about themselves and their ambitions, frustrations, accomplishments. And they like to be helpful in ways that enable them to feel potent."[20]

To get people to talk about themselves, ask questions such as, "The last time we were together you mentioned that you were going on a cruise. When did you get back? How was the trip?" Listen actively. Nod your head a little, say "uh huh," look interested. Make yourself be interested. People may know it if you are faking it too much.

As you listen to others, try to cue into ways that you could help them. They will often remember and return the favors. If someone helps you, immediately send a thank-you note. "When you're given a lead, a connection, or a valuable suggestion, the giver should immediately receive a handwritten thank-you note with a promise of reciprocal favors on demand."[21]

As you talk to others, don't be a whiner, a complainer, a naysayer all the time. No one needs another one of those in an organization.

After you've talked to someone for a while, introduce the person to someone else. Include some personal or professional information when introducing others so they have some topic to begin with. Example: "Robert, this is Julie Carlson. She just moved from Orlando to St.

Louis to become the Chief Medical Officer for ABC Hospital." Also, learn to tactfully break away from a conversation and meet others by introducing the other person to someone else and then moving away. You might say, "I'll call you next week" or "I have a few other people I need to talk to. I'll see you a little later."

Some logistical suggestions—at a cocktail party, hold your drink in your left hand so you can shake hands with your right hand. In today's society, anyone can offer the handshake first. Avoid messy food if you are truly trying to talk to people. Dripping ribs or chicken wings are just too difficult to manage. Carry fresh business cards in your pocket to offer when appropriate. People are offended if you are pushing business cards at everyone whether they ask for them or not, but you certainly want to have them on you. The easiest thing to do is have some loose ones in a pocket so you don't have to fumble for them.

"Don't attend one meeting, rush home, and assume you're on the road to a new job. Building useful relationships takes time....Speed the process by volunteering to work on a committee and by supplying your contacts with useful information."[21]

The following quote from *How to Fireproof Your Career* is valuable, not from the point of view of learning the labels but for showing the gradual building of relationships in the networking process: "Acquaintances are people you barely know. You bump into them in the cafeteria or at a Chamber of Commerce event, but you never see them again. Associates are people you see regularly because you have chosen to join in a group that brings you into contact with them at a professional association, an alumni club, or a volunteer activity. Over time, your associates experience you as someone who is energizing to be with, who can be counted on to come through with what he or she has promised, and who has valuable skills. Actors are the people on your list with whom you are actively exchanging valuable information and resources. You give them leads or tips. They tell you about a resource or introduce you to someone you want to meet....Giving with no strings attached is the way to invite reciprocity. Advocates are people who go out of their way to find opportunities to refer and recommend you to others. Allies care about your success. These relationships are long-term and usually turn into friendships as allies see each other socially, as well as professionally. You won't have time to cultivate too many relationships to this level, so you must select these people carefully. CAUTION; You'll be labeled a 'nuisance networker' for sure if, out of enthusiasm or urgency, you violate the natural development of trust in a relationship...by trying to jump from acquaintance to advocate or ally."[22]

When you are considering a career change, you will not only attend meetings, but also want to talk to as many people as you can in all areas of your life. Make yourself contact at least five people a month. If you are in a hurry to make a change, the number will be higher. To jog your memory, here is a list of the kinds of people you can contact:

- Other physicians in your area
- Physicians in the area you would like to move to
- Members of committees on which you serve
- Members of your professional society

- Medical school and undergraduate classmates
- Military colleagues
- Friends
- Family
- Lawyers
- Accountants
- Competitors

"Don't forget to call your university placement office and alumni association. Look through your synagogue or church [any house of worship], social organizations, health club, and any other directories you have that contain names of people you know or who might conceivably believe they know or have heard of you."[23]

Also, as part of the networking process, you will want to contact physician executive search firms. Get to know the recruiters that deal regularly with the sectors of the health care industry of interest to you. You can find a list of reputable firms by reading the on-line job postings on ACPE's website (Career Link) or by reading the classified ads in the back of the *Physician Executive Journal*.

Professional recruiters are excellent networkers and can help you find the job you want at no cost to you, as well as help you expand your network. These people will not immediately say to you that they will find you a job, because they work for the organization doing the hiring, not for the physician, but, if you tell them about yourself, they will keep you in mind as they try to fill their positions.

Figler uses an elaborate metaphor to describe the networking process: "Everyone has a friend who has a friend. Somewhere in that chain of friends, you are standing with your arms at your sides and your eyes closed. Now if you carefully open your eyes, reach out to the two friends waiting on either side, and grasp their hands firmly, you will feel the electricity of a personal contact network begin to course through your body. It will be stimulating, but not shocking. You will feel alive with the circuit of energy that comes from plugging into people networks. However, be aware that any time you drop your hands and close your eyes again, you have broken the connection. The life of the circuit depends on your ability to keep the switches open. I don't know how to help people who are asleep at the switch."[24]

Even if you are not literally holding the hands of people, you are making contact if you are talking to them. So get out there and talk—maybe more than you want to or are used to. Keep talking and increase your network.

Make networking a way of life. "'I tried networking last Thursday and nothing happened,' says Janice in frustration. Of course not. It's a process, not an event. Sure, you have to begin by putting specific events on your calendar, but the goal is to make connecting a way of life. It takes at least six months to cultivate a bountiful network."[25]

When you are doing the hard work of a job search, "keep a list of activities you enjoy to reward yourself with when you complete your daily or weekly activities....Take a nap, a hot bath, ride your bike, garden, make a cup of tea and sit outside and read for half an hour."[26]

A networking quiz, taken from *How to Fireproof Your Career* is at the end of this chapter.[27] It is not meant to make you feel bad about what you don't do, but I think it is an excellent reminder of the possibilities of things you can do to increase your network. Take the time to go through it and then score your performance in networking. If you're like most of us, improvement will be called for. You might try picking one new activity a month to increase your network.

References

1. Tyler, J. *Tyler's Guide: The Health Care Executive's Job Search*, Third Edition. Chicago, Ill.: Health Administration Press, 2002, p. 48.

2. Tiffan, W. "When Downsizing Points to You." Presentation at Perspectives in Medical Management, Chicago, Ill., May 1995.

3. Linney, B. "Bringing Reality to the Job Hunt Process." *Physician Executive* 22(1):53-5, Jan. 1996.

4. Cohn, G. "An Executive's Quest for a New Job Is a Lesson in Coolness and Strategy." *Wall Street Journal*, Nov. 19, 1985.

5. Marion, P. *Crisis Proof Your Career*. New York, N.Y.: Berkley Books, 1994, p. 167.

6. Tyler, L. CPE Tutorial Course, American College of Physician Executives, Tampa, Fla., Feb. 2006.

7. Navarro, A. http://www.worktransitions.com/wt_columns/col_0508.htm 10/ 17/2005. Work Transitions Business Journal columns, "Use Networking Interviews to Vet Your Candidacy," Aug. 2005.

8. Tyler, L. "Networking Strategies that Work." *Healthcare Executive* 9(3):38, May-June 1994.

9. Tyler, L. *Tyler's Guide: The Healthcare Executive's Job Search*, p. 53.

10. *Ibid.*, p. 49.

11. Tyler, L. "Networking Is Tough: Not Working Is Tougher." Healthcare Executive 11(1):36-7. Jan.-Feb. 1996.

12. Donna Vavala, Health Communication Consultant, Odessa, Fla., personal communication, 1996.

13. Tyler, J., *Tyler's Guide: The Healthcare Executive's Job Search*, p. 49.

14. Carnegie, D. *How to Win Friends and Influence People*. New York, N.Y.: Pocket Books, 1981, p. 94.

15. Kennedy, M. *Get the Job You Want and the Money You're Worth*. Tampa, Fla.: American College of Physician Executives, 1995, p. 7.

16. Tyler, L., CPE Tutorial, American College of Physician Executives, Feb 20, 2006, Tampa Fla.

17. Baber, A., and Waymon, L. *How to Fireproof Your Career. Survival Strategies for Volatile Times*. New York, N.Y.: Berkley Books, 1995, p. 201.

18. *Ibid.*, p. 208.

19. Kennedy, M., *op. cit.*, p. 6.

20. Figler, H. *The Complete Job Search Handbook*. New York, N.Y.: Henry Holt and Co., 1979, p. 190.

21. Kennedy, M., *op. cit.*, p. 8.

22. Baber, A., and Waymon, L., *op. cit.*, pp. 202-4.

23. Kennedy, M., *op. cit.*, p. 14.

24. Figler, H., *op. cit.*, p. 123.

25. Baber, A., and Waymon, L., *op. cit.*, p. 216.

26. Marion, P., *op. cit.*, p. 171.

27. Baber, A., and Waymon, L., *op. cit.*

Networking Quiz*

Circle yes (Y) or no (N) for each of the following questions.

Y N 1. I see all those informal conversations at business and social events as opportunities to use my small talk skills to build relationships and expand my network.

Y N 2. I know at least 50 people well enough (professionally or in the community) to call and say, "Hi, this is [my name]," and they know who I am and what my capabilities are.

Y N 3. People in my network have referred me to at least 10 people who have given me some kind of career or personal information.

Y N 4. I'm comfortable calling friends of friends, and friends of friends of friends to seek information.

Y N 5. I belong to at least four professional or community organizations and am visibly active in them.

Y N 6. I read two trade journals or magazines in my field and two general news publications consistently.

Y N 7. I know people outside of my profession from activities, such as sports, PTA, or volunteer work.

Y N 8. I've taken at least one course or gone to one convention to help me stay current in my field or learn about a new field.

Y N 9. I stay in touch with people I knew and worked with at previous jobs.

Y N 10. I make a point of meeting people outside my organization, profession, or industry, and at all levels of the hierarchy.

Y N 11. At a social or business event, I'm comfortable with introductions and can remember the names of people I meet.

Y   N   12. I introduce people to one another at business and social events.

Y   N   13. When people ask, "What do you do?" I avoid long, confusing job titles and labels. Instead I tell what I do, simply and vividly, by giving an example of a recent project or success.

Y   N   14. I let people know the kinds of problems I can solve, so that they can refer exactly the right kind of work challenges, job leads, or career information to me.

Y   N   15. When I talk to people, I usually find up-to-date information on something of professional or personal interest to me.

Y   N   16. I talk frequently with others for support, ideas, and resources.

Y   N   17. I systematically network with people in my organization who work in other departments, other divisions, and other locations.

Y   N   18. I have business cards and enjoy using conversation to look for ways to give or receive information or services so that exchanging cards is valuable and necessary.

Y   N   19. I always find a good way to say, "Thank you," when someone gives me information or resources or a referral to someone they know.

Y   N   20. I look for ways that my resources and information can help others fulfill their personal and professional goals.

Scoring yourself: Count how many times you circled Y, then analyze your score as follows:

1-10   Strengthen your career security as you learn the basics of networking. In the past, you may not have felt comfortable networking or may not have been convinced that networking could benefit you. However, you can learn how to do it, feel comfortable, and improve your on-the-job performance as well as your long-range career security.

11-14   You can give and get even more in your professional and personal networks as you develop your networking skills.

15-17   You have only a few gaps in your network.

18-20   Bravo! You're well on the way to experiencing the power of career security through networking.

* Adapted from Baber, A., and Waymon, L. *How to Fireproof Your Career. Survival Strategies for Volatile Times.* New York, N.Y.: Berkley Books, 1995, pp. 198-201.

Chapter Eight

Write a Powerful Resume

Most of us put off writing or updating a resume. It's sobering to review your work activities and put them in print. We are plagued with notions: Is it enough? Is that all there is? My whole life, and I'm supposed to put it on three pages—they must be crazy. Those considering career changes have to overcome the censoring voices and put together a resume (3 pages), not a curriculum vitae (CV-I've seen some that were more than 20 pages).

Everyone I have talked to, including recruiters, hates to read resumes as much as you hate to write them, so you need to grab the reader's attention right away using numbers. If you are the Chief Medical Officer of a 13-hospital system, you have done many great things that you may think the position title implies, but if you find yourself looking for another job, you must put on paper what you have accomplished in a short resume. If you just send a CV or bio without accomplishment statements, you might be cut from the first group of 12 that the recruiter presents to a client because the employer can't see evidence of your good works.

A natural inclination is to list what you are responsible for, but that is not enough. You need to tell the results of what you did.

Content

Here is an example of the difference between telling what your responsibilities are and telling your accomplishments:

Medical Director of Surgical Services

Wrong way:

Charged with responsibility of improving O.R. scheduling and reducing O.R. supply costs by consolidating suppliers and negotiating improved contracts.

Right way with numbers:

Decreased number of suppliers and established strategic relationships with new vendor base, resulting in 10% reduction in cost of supplies, extended terms, and on-time surgery starts which improved to 98% from 78%.[1]

The use of numbers is crucial. Think outside of health care for a moment. If you are a sales person in the linen department responsible for towels, you can rearrange them beautifully everyday, but until you sell ten towels, you don't have a measurable accomplishment.

"People don't read resumes. They skim them. If the first third of a resume doesn't grab them, they toss it."[2] "While there is no consensus on how to write the perfect resume, one thing is certain: you have just one minute to grab a potential employer's attention....[A] resume is a marketing brochure and you are the product."[3]

A resume is a short powerful document that showcases your accomplishments. It is a necessary document to use in a job search, but by itself it will not get you a job. "Warning! A resume is merely a facilitation tool; it is a first step, not an end in itself. Some job seekers believe that the preparation of a good resume is the most important part of their job search, but even the most stellar and professional resume does not ensure a job. In truth, a good interview is the most important....[A]s you embark on your job search, you will frequently be asked for your resume.... Without it, you cannot go to the next step, an interview."[4]

Randomly mailing resumes does not often get an interview for a high-level job. Word-of-mouth contact usually gets you the interview, but you must have a good-looking resume to send before you get there. It must look as polished as your interview suit and give the employer valuable information about you.

A curriculum vitae, which many people have, is a long document—as long as it needs to be, because it tells all the places you have shown up for work, all your publications, education, everything you have done. We all need one to keep track of our professional lives, but it is not what you send a potential employer. People doing the hiring do not want to read all about you. They're busy or lazy or bored by too much information. If we become the ones doing the hiring, we don't want to read long ones either.

So write a short, powerful resume to send to a potential employer—no more than three pages. That means you will have to pick and choose items from your curriculum vitae. Making it short forces you to put your best stuff down and leave out things you don't want to do again. Choose the activities that you have enjoyed doing in the past and would like to do more of in the future. Also, choose activities that are appropriate for the job you are applying for. If you want a management position, you would tell what you accomplished on a utilization review committee or how you improved patient safety rather than a great discovery you made in your clinical practice.

An exercise that can help you make these decisions is to make a two-part list of things you really love to do and things you do well. "Examples of things you love to do in one column could be leading a meeting, making a plan, adding columns of figures, working with patients, mentoring a young doctor. When you picture this task, you have a feeling in your gut—I really like that. In the second column, list what you do well. You have gotten feedback from people consistently that you do mentor people well or you do plan well. You may have a list of 10 or 20 things, but it won't go on forever because one part of the list will eliminate some things."[2]

Format

At the top of the first page of your resume, type your full name, address, home and office phone numbers (if it is all right for your office to know you are looking), cell phone if you check your voice messages regularly. Include zip code, area code, personal email. You do not want the employer to have to do the work of looking up that information. You provide all the information so they can easily get in touch with you.

Next, list your professional experience. It goes before education, because experience is the most important factor in getting a management position. You tell not only where you showed up for work and when (the items usually included in the CV), but also what you accomplished while you were there. People want to know most what you have been doing for the past three to five years, even though they want to read about all of your experience. If you have 20 years of experience, some information will have to be left out. When you choose items from your CV, most likely you will have to add information. True, you worked at St. Vincent's hospital from 2000 to 2005, but what did you do while you were there? Did you help lower costs in the emergency department? Tell how much. If you worked for a managed care facility, you might say: Developed four new satellite offices, recruited eight primary care physicians over a two-year period, and reduced the hospital utilization rate from 300 to 225 days per 1,000, which resulted in a first-time operational surplus for the plan.

Notice the numbers. People like to know that you have saved an organization money or increased its revenues, and they want to know how much and over what period. "[I]nclude the number of full-time employees (FTEs) supervised, the number of departments reporting to you, the total amount of the budget you directed, and the names of committees on which you served."[5] Use numbers to prove your general statements whenever you can.

Use strong active voice verbs, such as developed, recruited, reduced. An example of active voice is "John hit the ball." Passive voice is "The ball was hit by John." Stay away from the passive. Just as the name implies, it is not as powerful. Other action verbs: "chair, control, decrease, develop, direct, edit, establish, handle, implement, manage, negotiate, review, revise, supervise."[6] When applying for management positions, use some phrases, such as "led the team that," to show that you can manage people. Managers are not supposed to do everything themselves. They are supposed to help others to do.

A chronological format for your resume is best.. You list what you've done in reverse order. For example, your most recent job from 2003 to the present is listed first under professional experience. Then you describe the position you had from 1999 to 2003 and so on, heading backward.

If you are running out of room, you may have to leave out some information from 15 years ago, but you must account for all the years with a few explanatory words.

Examples: St. Vincents Hospital
            1997-1998 President of the Medical Staff
            1996-1998 Chair of Strategic Planning Committee.
            1996-1998 Chair of Hospital Utilization Review Committee

"The further you go back in time, the more important it is to condense your responsibilities and accomplishments. The general rule: Condense heavily the descriptions of jobs held prior to the 10-year mark."[7]

Many recruiters will change the order and format of your resume so the resumes of all the candidates they are submitting are uniform. But they will not do your work for you. You must present them a two- to three-page resume. Even though I've heard some recruiters say to list the education first, I still recommend that you list your professional management experience first, because that is what will get the recruiter's and hiring organization's attention quickest. If that fills the bill, they will continue reading.

Education can be listed in the order that it happened or in reverse chronological order, whichever you prefer. Most of your education was in college and medical school, but people do notice if you have management education if you are applying for a management position. The important concern for the education section is that you have the entry and completion date and the degree earned for each item. If it took you six years to finish college because you had to work to earn money, you need to mention that. Explain gaps of a year or longer, not months—that's getting too detailed.

What you include after work experience and education will be determined by how much room is left and what kind of position you are applying for. If you are applying for a management position, you would include publications on management topics, not your clinical publications. Many of those doing the hiring will look at a long list of clinical publications and say "So what—you're not going to be practicing cardiology now." If you are applying to be Dean of a Medical School, you can include all your publications in a separate attachment, because publications are the badge of honor in academic circles.

Do include licensure and board certification. Most medical management positions require board certification. People ask, "Why, since I won't be doing internal medicine." It may be like a dog needing a pedigree to be a show dog, or it may be that other doctors you manage will have passed the boards, and they want to know that you made it through boot camp too. Fair or not, it most often is a requirement.

You can include honors (Alpha Omega Alpha, Phi Beta Kappa), languages (Spanish is a plus these days), professional associations (American College of Physician Executives, American Academy of Pediatrics), or other information that you think is appropriate for the job you are applying for.

There is much debate about whether to include birth date. It's your choice. Recruiters have told me they can figure it out whether you put it or not. Recruiters have told me they are looking for people in the age range of 45-55. However, I have known younger and older physicians who got positions because of good networking contacts who felt they had enough drive and experience on the young side and enough energy and excitement as well as experience on the older side of the range.

If you have room, you can list interests: Gourmet cooking, coaching children's soccer, piano, golf, travel. I wouldn't put sky diving. The risk of that could be alarming to a potential employer

Do not put in the resume why you are leaving your present position, your personal opinions, and salary history. The interview is the place to discuss such things. Don't list your references or say they are available upon request. Everyone already knows you will provide references, and you are wasting words if you tell them they are available. Also, do not give the names of your references until you have called each one of them and asked his or her permission. You want a reference to be prepared to talk about you, not caught off guard.

Once you have collected all the information you need for the resume, you must think about how to dress up the finished product. People do pay attention to the color and thickness of the paper, the quality of the print. Just as you use fine linens on a dining table for important guests, you use fine quality paper to impress your potential employer. "Black type on white 24-lb. bond paper is still preferred. Use a 10-12 point (preferred) typeface in Times Roman or Helvetica and a laser printer."[8]

Even though all recruiters will want an electronic version of your resume to put in their data banks, you still need good looking hard copies when someone requests one and to take to the interview in case someone has misplaced theirs and asks for one.

The resume often has to be changed from one prospective employer to another. You may find you want to highlight certain of your activities based on what the employer says it is looking for. Any time your experience matches what they have listed in the job description, you have a better chance of being chosen to go for an interview.

Layout

Be consistent in your resume's layout. Put the headings for professional experience, education, and other main headings in bold print. "You could use uppercase letters to emphasize certain sections, but don't use underlining because of the rise of the practice of scanning resumes."[9]

I know you will want to use all the space for your information, but having enough white space makes others want to read the document. Have top, bottom, and side margins and a space between major items.

No typing mistakes. "Have the nit-pickiest person you know proof it. A misspelling or grammatical error could be fatal. It's also inexcusable."[10] If your resume has errors, people think you don't pay attention to details. Even with spell checkers on computers, it's almost impossible to catch all the typos yourself, because you've been working with the information so long you become blind to errors.

Cover Letter

A resume never leaves home without a cover letter, and every resume sent out has a different cover letter. Otherwise, the person receiving it looks at it and thinks several possible thoughts: What's this? Why did I get it? Why should I read another resume? It gets put in the trash can or is conveniently hidden under a pile so the recipient will not feel guilty about not reading it. The cover letter should tell briefly how you learned of the position, why you are sending your resume, and when you will call to see if you can meet with the person. It is written on the same paper that the resume is on. The cover letter is the last part in the writing process, and it is not written until you know exactly to whom you are sending the resume.

"If you are sending your resume to a search firm, you are probably one of 15 or 20 that they are looking at, because the search firm does the initial cut. Search firms are under no obligation to help you, because they are not in the business to find people jobs. They are in the business to be hired by companies to find people. How do they do it? By networking. Have a good cover letter that states what salary expectations you have, what you are looking for, and a few highlights from your career, but you don't need to repeat everything that's in your resume. When they receive the resume, someone will know what the current searches are. If it doesn't match any of the current searches, they put it aside. Don't expect to hear back from them unless they have an appropriate search under way. They are not going to call unless they have something hot."[2]

Recruiters I interviewed said they go straight to the resume looking for numbers and bypass the cover letter so don't make it a long document that gets in their way when they are in a hurry.

Voice Mail

If your resume lands in the right hands, don't blow it all by making it difficult for people to get in touch with you or have them be turned off by your answering service or machine. I have called some people in a job search where the phone rang forever with no answering service. That is not acceptable.

"It's important to have a professional, simple voice mail greeting when searching for a job. Over and over again, we hear things like 'Hi, I'm not here. Leave a message and if it's good, I might call you back.' This doesn't paint a good image...and we get it from all walks and levels of life."[11]

An appropriate message can be as simple as, "This is Dr. John Taylor. Please leave a message." Do not have children crying or dogs barking in the background of your message.

As much trouble as it is to write a resume, you feel a sense of accomplishment when you finish. You get a concrete look at who you are and what you've done professionally. As you make plans for your future, it is important to examine your present and past to see if the direction you are heading in makes sense. Preparing a resume allows you to place your life's accomplishments in order and it is step one in preparing for the interview.

References

1. Grebenschikoff, J. Presentation at Spring Institute, American College of Physician Executives, Boston, Mass., 2005.

2. Tiffan, W. "When Downsizing Points to You." Presentation at ACPE Perspectives in Medical Management, Chicago, Ill., May 1995.

3. Marion, P. *Crisis Proof Your Career*. New York, N.Y.: Berkley Books, 1994, p. 169.

4. Tyler, J. *The Health Care Executive's Job Search, 3rd ed.* Chicago, Ill.: Health Administration Press, 2002, p. 3.

5. Tyler, J. *The Health Care Executive's Job Search, 3rd edition.* Chicago, Ill.: Health Administration Press, 2002, p. 8.

6. *Ibid.*, p. 13.

7. *Ibid.*, p. 7.

8. Kennedy, M. *Get the Job You Want and the Money You're Worth*. Tampa, Fla.: American College of Physician Executives, 1995, p. 17.

9. Tyler, L., *op. cit.*, p. 5.

10. *Ibid.*, p. 18.

11. Bill Fries, President of ATS Staffing, Tampa, Fla., Email, Jan. 13, 2006.

Sample Resume

John Smith, Jr., MD, MBA, CPE
Rockport, Michigan
xxx-xxx-xxxx (home)
xxx-xxx-xxxx (work)
xxx-xxx-xxxx (cell)
johnsmith@yahoo.com

PROFESSIONAL EXPERIENCE

2003-Present
Healing Hospital, Rockport, Michigan
350 bed not-for-profit hospital with a medical staff of 400

Vice President Medical Affairs

- Improved patient satisfaction rating from 83.3% in 2003 to 86.3% in 2004 and 89.2% in 2005.
- Implemented successful advanced appointment access. Achieved same day access in primary care clinic.
- Enhanced use of electronic medical record so that 93% of orders are completed electronically, and 83 % of progress notes are signed within two days (2005)
- Implemented disease management programs for congestive heart failure, coronary artery disease, diabetes, high risk maternity, and chronic obstructive pulmonary disease.
- Participated in facilities planning process culminating in construction of an ambulatory care center.
- Helped department chairs confront disruptive physicians resulting in improved behavior for four and suspension of privileges for one.
- Led patient safety initiatives. Developed program to increase hand washing and decrease falls.
- Reorganized quality efforts to address issues of accountability to the Board of Directors. Established the council on Quality including six Board members to collect data and implement improvements.

1999-2003
Northside Hospital, 300 bed community hospital, Shore Lake, Illinois

- Served as President of the Medical Staff. Fully restructured the medical board to improve clinical and performance outcomes as well as patient satisfaction.
- Chair of the Medical Board. Expanded the traditional responsibilities of the position to include being a major liaison between CEO and administrative staff, the medical staff, nursing and allied health staff.
- Integrated Utilization Management into department activities resulting in 22% reduction in bed days of care.

- Encouraged department use of performance data in re-credentialing activities.
- Comprehensively updated the Medical Staff Bylaws. Used information technology to document staff concurrence. The bylaws passed JCAHO survey without objection.
- Brought harmonious resolution to several personnel issues involving difficult medical staff members.

1994-2003
Jamison Medical Group-75 physician multi-specialty group, Shore Lake, Illinois.
- Practiced Internal Medicine
- Served on Quality Improvement Committee, Credentialling and Privileging committees (1996-2000)
- Facilitated Strategic planning retreat for group. (2001)
- Served on Board of Directors (2000-2003)

EDUCATION

2002-2004   University of Massachusetts at Amherst, MBA

1991-1994   Residency Program in Internal Medicine, Montefiore Medical Center, Bronx, NY, Chief Resident 1993-1994

1987-1991   University of Virginia School of Medicine, Charlottesville, VA, MD

1983-1987   University of Pennsylvania College of Arts and Sciences, Philadelphia, PA, BA in English

CERTIFICATION

1996   Diplomate, American Board of Internal Medicine

2005   Certified Physician Executive

LICENSURE

Illinois
Michigan

PROFESSIONAL ASSOCIATIONS

American College of Physician Executives
American College of Healthcare Executives
American Society of Internal Medicine

Sample Resume *(more experienced physician executive)*

JAMES J. MOORE, MD, MMM, CPE, FACPE
350 LINCOLN DR.
THOMASVILLE, MD 32148

Home: xxx-xxx-xxxx   Work: xxx-xxx-xxxx
e-mail: tmoore@rr.com   Fax: xxx-xxx-xxxx

PROFESSIONAL EXPERIENCE

THOMASVILLE MEDICAL CENTER, Thomasville, MD (July 1999 to present)

(355 bed community not-for-profit teaching hospital with 2,000+ employees and annual revenues of $185 million)

Senior Vice President and Chief Medical Officer

- Implemented clinical improvement task forces culminating in recognition as one of the 2004 Solucient Top 100 Performance Improvement Leaders nationally.

- Initiated hospital-wide clinical documentation program based on Milliman & Robertson (M&R) criteria, resulting in a managed care denial rate of 2.7% in 2004 and a reduction of $2 million in denials from 2002.

- Attained and actively maintained medical center as one of the top five lowest LOS and expense per adjusted discharge hospitals per the Maryland Hospital Association Financial and Statistical (FAST) Report.

- Effected significant restructuring of Medical Staff Governance/Bylaws to better align with strategic growth initiatives by eliminating barriers to physician entry and resulting in 26% medical staff growth since 1999.

- Actualized hospital wide patient safety programs, resulting in significant compliance with Leap Frog Group criteria, JCAHO Patient Safety Standards and National Quality Forum 30 Patient Safety Practices.

- Led movement of medical center from bottom two quartiles in 16 PRO clinical indicators in 2003 for heart disease, pneumonia and surgical infection prevention to the top quartile by 2005.

THE GREELEY COMPANY, Marblehead, MA (January 2005 to present)

(A nationally respected consulting and training company known for providing practical, effective strategies and solutions to assist the leaders of today's health care organizations; an industry authority in heath care regulation and compliance and medical staff development and effectiveness)

Senior Health Care Consultant (part-time)

- Led medical staff effectiveness seminars and training for health system boards and medical staffs to understand and achieve clearly delineated lines of authority and responsibility.

- Assessed and implemented changes required to enhance medical staff effectiveness in carrying out accountabilities for health care quality.

- Implemented medical staff governance change through redesign of medical staff structure, processes and bylaws.

- Conducted in-depth JCAHO preparedness surveys and implemented JCAHO corrective action plans in organizations facing denial of unconditional accreditation.

- Augmented medical staff leadership through active education and on-site intervention with hospital and health system medical staffs.

JONES MEDICAL CENTER, Richmond, VA (January 1998 to June 1999)

(225 bed not-for-profit medical center with 1,000 employees and annual revenues in excess of $74 million)

Vice President, Medical Affairs

- Initiated physician driven Clinical Resource Management project that eliminated $5 million annual expense while maintaining quality in institution facing negative operating margin.
- Created new Case Management and Performance Improvement infrastructure to support the Clinical Resource Management endeavor.
- Led medical quality program for disease management initiatives.
- Significantly participated in strategic planning and business initiatives to identify and implement services/sites/alliances for a fuller continuum of care.
- Assumed interface role in wide chasm between Medical Staff leadership, Administration and hospital Board by focusing on clinically driven, mutually beneficial business initiatives.

WILSON REGIONAL MEDICAL CENTER, Wilson, NC (February 1997 to December 1997)

(314 bed county authority medical center with 1,500 employees, annual operating revenues in excess of $130 million; an integrated delivery system including tertiary cardiac services)

Vice President, Medical Affairs

ROSE MEMORIAL HOSPITAL, Albany, NY (November 1995 to January 1997)

(130 bed non-profit medical center with 500 employees and annual operating revenues in excess of $30 million; member of NorthLink, a consortium of eleven health care providers for joint ventures and network formation)

Vice President, Medical Affairs

ST. JOSEPH'S MEDICAL CENTER, Springfield, IL (July 1980 to October 1995)

(475 bed, 3 campus medical center with 2,000 employees and annual revenues in excess of $90 million)

Practicing Physician, Progressive Medical Staff Leadership Positions including President of the Medical Staff

PROFESSIONAL PRACTICE

- Springfield Neurological Associates, Springfield, IL (1980 to 1995)

EDUCATION

- Masters in Medical Management, Tulane University, New Orleans, Louisiana (2002)
- MD Degree, Johns Hopkins University, Baltimore, MD (1975)
- Bachelor of Arts, University of Richmond, Richmond, VA (1971)

BOARD CERTIFICATION AND MEDICAL LICENSE

- Certified Physician Executive (CPE), Certifying Commission in Medical Management, Certificate 399
- Diplomate in Neurology, American Board of Psychiatry and Neurology
- Medical License—Maryland, Illinois, New York, North Carolina

Chapter Nine

Interviewing for a Position

The interview may be the barrier that stands between you and your exciting new career. It's a time when we all want to seem intelligent, charming, eloquent, and full of dazzling stories of great achievements. But, in fact, many interviewees have experienced anxiety that left them stuttering over answers or chattering aimlessly trying to calm themselves. Some people who can do a job quite well do not get it because they do poorly in interviews. Preparing ahead of time and practicing the interview will give you the best chance of making a good first impression on an organization.

Prepare

You prepare ahead of time by doing research and learning all you can about your potential employer.

- Join professional societies or trade associations, go to the meetings, and talk to physician members. Ask them about the work climate in their organizations. Here are examples of questions you might ask.
  - How are physician managers regarded by nonphysician executives?
  - If you are interested in a national or regional organization, find out who makes the decisions. Will you have any power in the local organization, or will all final decisions be made somewhere else? Will that bother you? Will top management want to hear your innovative ideas?
  - Does the organization have a history of frequently replacing top-level managers?
  - Can you advance in the organization?
  - If the organization has religious ties, do you need to be a part of that faith community or go along with its tenets? Are you willing to do that?
  - Does the physician executive (VPMA, CMO, Medical Director) have the power to make decisions, or is he or she just doing tasks that the doctors in the group do not want to do?
- Read journals and magazines that discuss the kind of management job you want. Every trade association and professional society has its own journal. Examples of journals that discuss management issues:

Health Leaders (Health Leaders Media)

Group Practice Journal (American Group Practice Association)

Modern Healthcare (Crain Communications)

Managed Care Magazine (Medimedia USA)

Physician Executive Journal (American College of Physician Executives)

American Medical News (American Medical Association)

Harvard Business Review

Call people you know in the organization. If you are interested in a management position and you know a cardiologist in a group, call the person and ask how he or she sees the role of the present physician executives. If calling people and asking them questions is difficult for you, write out everything you are going to say and have it by the phone. But talk in a voice that does not sound as if you are reading.

"In the job search, you need to get used to the idea that people really rely on first impressions. Whatever you can do in the first minutes with somebody is important. Take time to script what you are going to say on a voice mail. Stand up and smile and have a script that is right to the point. So and so referred me to you, I've had x years doing such and such, and you have a mini commercial about yourself. When you listen to a voice mail message, you have a picture in your mind about what that person is like. The same is true when you are on the phone. All of that practicing and rehearsing is the kind of thing we do with people in our program and you need to get used to doing it in preparing yourself."[1]

Jeff Taylor, founder of monster.com says, "You have ninety seconds to make a first impression. What can you say that will grab their interest and make them ask for more? You need to relate your key messages, plus just enough additional information to get them hooked."[2]

I have listened to voices on voice mail that were low, mumbly, and rambling and made an immediate judgment that this person could not do the job. I know it may not be true, but others also make the same judgment and won't call you back or look at your resume.

Read anything that you can find about the organization or the particular area of health care that you will be interviewing for. "Your first, and probably most important, step to getting the job you want and the salary you're worth is research....Please make friends with the reference room librarian and plan to cultivate and maintain this relationship indefinitely. Pick the library branch you frequent on the basis of this person's skills and helpfulness."[3]

Use the Internet to research a organization. Here are some places to start:

- Google—Type in www.google.com in the address line of your browser. Then type the organization or hiring manager's name in the search box. All kinds of articles will come up.
- Look at the organization's own website.

- Hoovers.com—Identifies key people in the company.
- http://news.surfwax.com/hospitals/—Gives numerous articles that have appeared in newspapers about the organization.
- Dun and Bradstreet—Business Background Report provides summary information on the operations, history, and background of a company and its senior management.

Call the public relations department and ask for the annual report and any brochures or publications that describe the organization. If it does not have a public relations department, ask the person who is scheduling the interview for you for any information he or she has on the organization.

Ask for in-house newspapers and magazines that give the good news about the organization. Read the local newspaper to see if some negative news appears.

Ask someone for an information interview. Using your network, find the name of someone in the organization you can talk to who might describe the work, personalities, or politics of the company.

- Ask for 15-20 minutes of the person's time so he or she will know that you do not plan to tie the person up for long.
- Ask, "How are you?" Listen to the answer. If the person replies in a frantic way, "Busy, busy, busy," that tells you something about the organization or the work style that is needed to fill the job.
- Tell the person you have three questions you would like to ask. Examples: How is the medical director (Chief Medical Officer, Vice President of Medical Affairs) viewed by top management? How is the organization doing financially? How do the doctors regard the medical director position?
- Listen carefully as the person decides what other subjects to cover.

Watching television one night, I saw an example of great results from an information interview. Alec Guinness at 20 wanted to be an actor but didn't know how to go about it. After watching John Gielgud in the same play for three performances, Guinness called him and asked him how he could become an actor. Gielgud said you need an acting teacher. Guinness hired a teacher, and, a year later, Gielgud gave him his first part in Hamlet. In addition to working with an acting coach, Guinness had watched Hamlet 150 times. He had effectively sought information and then he did his homework.

During the Interview

During the interview you will give examples of what you have accomplished in your previous positions. Daniel Pink in *A Whole New Mind* quotes Alan Kay, "Scratch the surface in a typical boardroom and we're all just cavemen with briefcases, hungry for a wise person to tell us stories."[4] Your examples need to be good, short stories with numbers whenever possible. They want to know how you are going to make life in their organization better.

During the interview you need to convey:

- How you can help the organization make or save money. Example: "As medical director, I believe that I can help your organization reduce hospital utilization by 20 percent without sacrificing quality."

- Specific examples of your achievements in previous positions, each delivered in no more than a one-minute "minicase history" (focused on results, not activity). Example: "During my past two years as director of strategic planning and development, we opened four new satellite offices and developed two new departments in the main office."

- Knowledge of the industry (marketplace, products, personal contacts, inside and outside pressures). Example: "The contacts that I have made in my previous national organization as well as in two national professional societies have helped me to understand the competition in managed care."

- Knowledge of the potential employer's company (including its goals, challenges, history, and top management). Example: "I am aware that ABC Hospital intends to be one of the largest systems in the area in the next five years. I believe that my experience in development and contacts in the industry can help you realize your goal."

Potential Interview Questions

The following is a list of questions that are often asked in interviews. Take the time to fully write out answers to them before you go for the interview. You will not take your notes with you, but the information will be with you because you have so thoroughly thought it out.

- Tell me briefly what you've been doing since medical school.

- Why are you looking for a job?

- Why did you leave your last job?

- What were your major responsibilities in your last job?

- What are your greatest strength and your greatest weakness? (Try to couch the weakness in a positive light. Example: "I've been told that sometimes I'm too compassionate with subordinates." You can sometimes say your weakness is your strength taken too far. Example: "I'm very organized, but occasionally I'm so organized it slows me down. When that happens, I reassess the situation and speed things up.")

- What are your long- and short-term goals? Example of long-term—Become CEO of a health care organization. Example of short- term—Develop expertise in utilization management.

- What are the three greatest accomplishments in your career? Example: Led organization as it changed from being a local health care provider to a regional provider.

- What kind of contribution can you make to our company? Example: I believe I can organize and energize the medical staff so that its members would feel more supportive of the goals of the organization.

- How do you react to criticism?

- Describe a time when you made a big mistake and how you handled it.

- Can you give me an example of how you have managed people in the past?

- How will your spouse feel about your taking this job, about relocating, about your work-related travel? (You may not be asked this directly in the interview, but at some point, it will come up in the social functions.)

- Have you ever hired or fired someone?

- Why do you want a career in management?

- How would you deal with a physician who is not performing well?

- Describe your experience with utilization review and quality assurance.

- How might you bridge the communication gap between physicians and administrators?

- Can you describe a time when you analyzed a problem, set a goal, created strategies for solving the problem, implemented the plan, and evaluated the results?

Tyler ok has an even more detailed list of questions that recruiters will ask on their first screening interview before you are selected to be interviewed by the organization.[5]

Illegal Questions

"Because of the Equal Employment Opportunity commission's efforts to end discriminatory practices, certain questions are out of bounds. Unfortunately, you still may be asked a blatantly illegal questions during an interview or in the first few weeks in a new position. However, in the interview setting when you want a position, you risk negative results if you challenge the interviewer on an out-of-bounds question."[6]

If you are good at handling humor, Tyler suggests some clever responses:

- "You know, mother told me that you wouldn't have the nerve to ask me that question."

- "One of my friends told me she was asked a similar question, and she just chuckled and asked if it were a mock interview."

- "I know you are kidding, so I'll go ahead to your next question."[6]

If those would not be comfortable for you, here are some simpler answers. Are you planning to have children? Not now. How will you take care of your children? I have a nanny who will be moving with me. The point is you may be asked these questions and if you want the interview process to continue, you cannot give a lecture about the illegalities of the question. Whatever your answer is to questions that you think you might be asked, practice it ahead of time so you can move smoothly through it.

"If you were unemployed for several months or even a year, be prepared to convince an interviewer that you weren't malingering or on a world tour. A gap is not an automatic knockout, because health care is in flux and some 40 percent of working adults have lost (and gained) jobs since 1990."[7]

"More organizations are doing telephone prescreening, serial interviews, group interviews, and reinterviews, but fewer are using stress interviews....About telephone prescreening....This is it—show time—the first interview. Stand up, gesture with your hands, and put enthusiasm and vitality into your voice. You can be out if you come across as dull on the phone."[8]

Practice the Interview

Get a video camera, read the answers to some of your interview preparation questions, and take a good look at yourself. Kennedy says, "You need access to a VCR and a camera or to a camcorder for practice interviewing. If you haven't interviewed within the past 6 to 12 months, this is essential. Practice will increase your confidence if you have what you believe to be 'handicaps,' e.g., you've been fired, have been unemployed for more than three months, or are unlikely to receive a positive reference from your current boss."[9] "Record yourself answering every nasty, intimidating, or merely embarrassing question your helper can think up. Do this in one-minute segments and then play it back. In four sessions, you will be measurably improved. There is no coaching like video."[10]

If you need to change something, keep trying it in front of the camera until you are satisfied. Also look at a video of someone you admire and notice what they do with their hands, eyes, voice, face. Try to copy the person.

An interviewer is influenced as much by what you don't say as by what you do say. Facial expression communicates much more than you may realize. How do you hold your face? Do you look pleasant or grim? Relaxed or uptight? Do you sound confident but not arrogant or argumentative? Do you sit up straight, walk holding yourself up—not slouched over, looking meek. Do you have a firm handshake but not one that breaks knuckles? Do you have a sarcastic sneer more than you realize? A pleasant expression with an occasional smile conveys confidence.

When we are nervous, or even bored, we all exhibit certain comforting behaviors. We pat ourselves, scratch, shift in our seats, but watch how much you do them. I saw a female physician in a meeting comb her hair, get out a mirror and put on lipstick, take her shoe off and rub her foot, push to get the shoe back on her foot. This behavior should have stopped in public when a teacher called you on it in the eighth grade or when your mother hounded you about it until you gave it up around everyone but her. This behavior does not exude confidence. Don't do it, especially in an interview.

The sound of your voice is also important. Is it too soft or too loud? Do you always sound as if you are giving orders? Do you sound as if you could never give orders? Neither extreme is effective for management jobs. You need a confident, firm voice that can get forceful but that can also be soft when appropriate. If you are serious about this, you will have to ask some people what they think. Individual coaching is often quite helpful.

Most people are nervous during an interview, especially at the beginning. You can use some of that energy to help you perform well, but, if you are excessively nervous, you need to prac- tice ways to relax. Purchase a relaxation tape and do it every day for three weeks. Your body will learn to relax and breathe slowly. If you get nervous during the actual interview, take a slow deep breath that is not noticeable and you will find you will calm down. Expect some nervousness, and use the energy it provides to make you alert and energetic.

On the day of the interview, arrive 5-10 minutes early, wearing clothes appropriate for the job, the company, and the industry culture. When in doubt, wear a conservative suit. For women, dark tailored suits with nothing low-cut at the neck and no extremely short skirts. For men, dark suits with ties that are not overly flashy. Recruiters tell me skirted suits are still the most conservative and widely accepted outfit for women. If, during the first inter- view, you notice female executives in pant suits, then you could wear a good, dark colored pant suit for the second interview.

Women: Your coat must be longer than your suit skirt. Men: Your coat must come below your knees. "Suburban" coats for men (just above the knee) haven't been appropriate for any business since the '60s. You'd have to sneak it into the Salvation Army pickup box to get rid of it."[11]

During the interview sit up straight, speak clearly, and look at the interviewer. Don't fiddle with your hair, glasses, a pen, or clothing.

Don't chew gum in public unless you are a very discreet chewer. I've seen a few people who are able to move their mouths once every 5 minutes. I chew like a cow chewing her cud and pop it on every munch. A woman who took care of me as a child taught me to do this when I was five, and I felt enormously accomplished once I learned it. As an adult it has made chewing gum unacceptable behavior even in front of family members.

Don't argue with your interviewer. If you do, you probably will not get the job. Do not crit- icize former employees, bosses, or co-workers. If you do, the interviewer thinks you may do the same about him or her someday.

Be concise. Don't over explain. If in doubt, ask, "Is that what you wanted to know?" Ask questions at the appropriate time about your job responsibilities, management practices, the assignments of co-workers, and performance evaluations (how often, with whom, how done). Usually, near the end of the interview, you'll be asked if you have any questions. It's fine to have this list written down. "It is appropriate and sound practice to discuss advancement potential, job descriptions, and evaluation procedures during an employ- ment interview."[12]

Two good questions to ask of everyone are "What is it like to work for the hiring manager? What do you hope I will accomplish in the first six months?"[13]

Be confident, but not arrogant. Arrogance often comes across in your tone of voice. Arrogance is very hard to explain with words, but extremely easy to hear with the ear. If every sentence has the same tune and you tend to go up in pitch at the end of most sentences, that might result in an arrogant sound. The only way to find out about this is to ask someone you think will be honest with you. If inside your head you are secretly thinking you're better than the people you contact, there is a good chance it is going to come out in the look on your face and the sound of your voice.

Don't sound desperate. A helpful attitude is described by Richard Bolles: "The job-interview is not a test, where the employer decides whether you pass or fail. It is part of their data-collecting, and—more importantly—part of your data-collecting too, since you should be still trying to decide if this is a good place for you to work, or not. In other words, the interview resembles dating more than it resembles someone buying a used car (you)."[14]

Let the employer bring up the issue of salary, but have in mind the lowest amount you would work for. Find out what people in similar positions are paid in that area of the country before you go to the interview so that you can know if the employer is being reasonable. Two organizations publish surveys of salary information for physician executives—Cejka Search/ American College of Physician Executives and Physician Executive Management Center.

Write a thank-you letter the day after the interview. Sending a thank-you note to anyone who is helpful anytime helps your career, but it is vital during the interview process. If your handwriting is good, a handwritten note is wonderful, but a typed letter or email is also acceptable. Do it quickly and make all the messages different if you have been interviewed by eight people. They will all end up in your file, and you don't want anyone to see that you sent the same note to everyone.

Comment on something good that happened in the interview. Mention that you would like to work for the company. Reiterate or tell another reason why you think you can help the organization meet its goals. In the note you might say, "'After our discussion I'm more convinced than ever that XYZ and I would be a good fit'....Say that you'll be calling in the next few days to see if the organization has made a decision. Then call as you said you would. Talk to the secretary if the decision maker isn't there. Better still, ask for voice mail and leave a detailed message. Persistence pays off!"[15]

Kennedy recommends that you "call back every 10 days, probably every other Friday."[16] "Job hunters tend to see unreturned telephone calls as a sign of impending rejection rather than as carelessness, work overload, a snafu in the system, or simply the desire to put off a difficult decision. Impute no motive to unreturned calls. Call until you get through. Always talk to the secretary as if she were an ally and leave a voice mail message....Persistent, low-pressure wooing works best."[17] "If you can't reach any of the people you interviewed with, beginning with the prospective boss or personnel person, leave messages with their secretaries or voice mail. Explain that you're very interested in the job and that you're inquiring to see if a decision has been made or when one may be....don't apologize for calling or suggest that you're being a nuisance."[18] "Continue to check back regularly. Don't slack off on other targets. You can be rejected after six interviews."[19]

After the interview, how do you stand the waiting? You try to go on with your life, but every minute you are not doing a specific task your mind goes back like a homing pigeon: Did I get the job? Did I get the house? You wonder and worry. Is this the right thing to do? Is it fair to others in the family? What if it doesn't work out? What will we do?

How do you cope? As much as possible, turn your attention to other things while you wait between the action steps. Keep telling people you are looking; contact other search firms. A retainer firm can only recommend you for one job at a time. Look at more than one job, more than one house, so you have options. This is very hard to do, because we tend to settle in on one thing we like and constantly ruminate about that one. "If you are serious about changing jobs and want to keep your momentum, not to mention your sanity and perspective, continue to interview right up until you accept an offer and give notice. If you don't, the importance of one near offer can be so magnified you will begin to believe that not getting the offer is the equivalent to career death. Even if you were 75/25 going in, you'll decide you must have this job. Don't put yourself under that kind of pressure."[20]

Plan on several interviews. "Certainly physicians who are getting ready to change from clinical careers to full-time management should probably interview for several positions before deciding on the right job, especially if they are going to have to make a geographic move. If a health care organization thinks enough of you to offer to pay your expenses to come for an initial interview, recruiters tell us that it is all right to go for that initial interview if you are more than 50 percent interested in the job. If you or your spouse is totally closed to living in that city or working for that organization, then it is not appropriate for you to interview for the position at the organization's expense. On the other hand, if you have doubts, but are open to the possibility, it is perfectly all right to go for that initial interview."[21]

Jennifer Grebenschikoff of the Physician Executive Management Center says, "Most health care organizations interview between three and five candidates in the first round of interviews. After that first round, the organization has usually narrowed the list either to one choice or possibly to two finalists, and, in that case, they will invite both finalists back for second interviews. Also, a physician should never take a job and the organization should never make a formal offer unless the spouse has had at least one visit to that new community."[22]

Employers want to hire enthusiastic people with good communication skills who will work hard. The interview is the place you can show them you have these qualities.

References

1. Tiffan, W. "When Downsizing Points to You." ACPE Perspectives in Medical Management, Chicago, Ill., May 1995.

2. Taylor, J. *Monster Careers*. New York, N.Y.: Penguin, 2004.

3. Kennedy, M. *Get the Job You Want and the Money You're Worth*. Tampa, Fla.: American College of Physician Executives, 1995, p. 4.

4. *Ibid.*, p. 5.

5. Tyler L. *Health Care Executive Search*, 3rd Edition, Chicago, Ill.: Health Administration Press, 2002, pp. 112-7.

6. *Ibid.*, p. 96.

7. Kennedy, M., *op. cit..*, p. 17.

8. *Ibid.*, p. 21.

9. *Ibid.*, p. 1.

10. *Ibid.*, p. 31.

11. *Ibid.*, p. 3.

12. Hartfield, J. In *Physicians in Managed Care. A Career Guide*, Bloomberg, M., and Mohlie, S., Editors. Tampa, Fla.: American College of Physician Executives, 1994, p. 77.

13. Tyler, L., CPE Tutorial, American College of Physician Executives, Tampa, Fla., Feb. 20, 2006.

14. Bolles, R. *The 2006 What Color Is Your Parachute?* Berkeley, Calif.: Ten Speed Press, 2006, p. 275.

15. Kennedy, M., *op. cit.*, p. 25.

16. *Ibid.*, p. 37.

17. *Ibid.*, p. 36.

18. *Ibid.*, p. 35.

19. *Ibid.*, p. 24.

20. *Ibid.*, p. 35.

21. George Linney Jr., MD, FACPE, Vice President, Tyler and Company, personal communication, 2006.

22. Jennifer Grebenschikoff, Vice President, Physician Executive Management Center, personal communication, 2006.

Further Reading

Baxter, R., and Brashear, M. *Do-It-Yourself Career Kit*. Moraga, Calif.: Bridgewater Press, 1990.

Bolles, R. *The 1985 What Color Is Your Parachute?* Berkeley, Calif.: Ten Speed Press, 1985.

Figler, H. *The Complete Job-Search Handbook*. New York, N.Y.: Henry Holt and Company, 1979.

Steward, C., and Cash, W. *Interviewing Principles and Practices*. Dubuque, Iowa: William. C. Brown Publishers, 1988.

Work Sheets

Potential interview questions:

Tell me briefly what you've been doing since medical school.

_____

_____

_____

_____

_____

_____

Why are you looking for a job?

_____

_____

_____

_____

_____

Why did you leave your last job?

_____

_____

_____

_____

_____

What were your major responsibilities in your last job?

_____

_____

_____

_____

_____

What is your greatest strength and your greatest weakness? (*Try to couch the weakness in a positive light. Example: I've been told that sometimes I'm too compassionate with subordinates.*)

Greatest strength _____

_____

_____

_____

Greatest weakness _____

_____

_____

_____

What are your long- and short-term goals? Example of long-term—Become CEO of a health care organization. Example of short-term—Develop expertise in utilization management.

Long-term goals _____

_____

_____

_____

_____

Short-term goals _____

_____

_____

_____

What are the three greatest accomplishments in your career? Example: Led organization as it changed from being a local health care provider to a regional provider.

1. _____

_____

2. _____

_____

3. _____

_____

What kind of contribution can you make to our company? Example: I believe I can organize and energize the medical staff so that its members would feel more supportive of the goals of the company.

_____

_____

_____

_____

_____

_____

How do you react to criticism?

_____

_____

_____

_____

_____

_____

_____

Describe a time when you made a big mistake and how you handled it.

_____

_____

_____

_____

_____

Can you give me an example of how you have managed people in the past?

_____

_____

_____

_____

_____

_____

How will your spouse feel about your taking this job, about relocating, about your work-related travel?

_____

_____

_____

_____

_____

_____

Have you ever hired or fired someone?

_____

_____

_____

_____

_____

Why do you want a career in management?

_____

_____

_____

_____

_____

How would you deal with a physician who is not performing well?

_____

_____

_____

_____

_____

Describe your experience with utilization review and quality assurance.

_____

_____

_____

_____

How might you bridge the communication gap between physicians and administrators?

_____

_____

_____

_____

_____

_____

_____

_____

Can you describe a time when you analyzed a problem, set a goal, created strategies for solving the problem, implemented the plan, and evaluated the results?

_____

_____

_____

_____

_____

_____

_____

_____

Chapter Ten

Negotiating Your Salary

The idea of negotiation raises the anxiety level of all but a few people, those who thrive on the thrill of competitive bargaining. Most physicians I've met do not relish the process and view it as a type of conflict. "Most of us react to conflict the same way our ancient ancestors reacted to saber-toothed tigers appearing on the horizon. Our instinct is still 'fight or flight,' however much we have evolved in other areas. Our primitive urge is either to fight back and escalate the conflict, or to run away. This flight may mean actually leaving the room, or simply withdrawing emotionally. When you give in to either fight or flight, you lose control of the situation and are likely to feel either abusive or victimized."[1] Kennedy says, " Unless you're prepared to overcome a natural reluctance to make counteroffers (in a negotiation), your options are not just limited, they're nonexistent."[2] "[O]ne of the rules…is, 'Get the money up front.'"[3]

I interviewed Bettina Kilbourne, who was offered less than she wanted for her first physician executive job. She asked a friend who was a recruiter to coach her through the process. The recruiter said, "Remember, they can afford more than that." Kilbourne says, "Women have to be especially careful that they don't get sucked into trying to take care of everyone's needs and thinking, "Oh well, gosh. If they really don't have the budget, blah, blah, blah." In a negotiating situation, the "nurturing" approach is inappropriate. It doubly arms the person with whom you are negotiating salary and terms.

"Employment negotiations are complex not only because there are so many potential items to negotiate but also because you need to maintain a good relationship with your future employer during the process….Mutual respect needs to be maintained throughout the negotiating process. If something goes wrong at this stage, it could jeopardize the offer of employment or you could end up wishing you had never accepted the position."[4]

In order to curb the inclination to fight or flee, determine what you want before you get into an important negotiation. It is even better if you write down your desires. You will get clear on what you want much quicker and you will remember the points better when you talk to the other person. Try to stick with honestly saying to yourself what you want rather than veering off in all directions about what you should want.

"[Y]ou are negotiating not just a salary but a package, which may include such things as salary, bonus, vacation, educational leave, insurance (health, life, dental, disability are possibilities), flexible hours, child care or elder care leave, flexible benefit plans, retirement plans, and relocation packages."[4] Other benefits you might ask for are paying dues for one specialty society and one management association, car or allowance for a car if your job requires lots of travel, assistance with buying out a malpractice tail, and a severance package. A position with a relatively high salary and no benefits may not answer your needs, despite the attractive salary. On the other hand, if the benefits are very generous and fit your needs, you may be willing to take a somewhat lesser salary."[4]

You need to know what other people are getting paid for jobs similar to yours. This requires research. Cejka Search and ACPE publish a compensation survey every two years. The Physician Executive Management Center, an executive search firm in Tampa, Florida, also publishes one.

Kennedy recommends you also do your own survey. Call people and say, "'I need to get an idea of what your organization would (does) pay for that job; when I've finished my survey, I'll send you a copy.'...Also talk with headhunters, look at industry surveys, do a literature search at the library, network out of town. The key is to establish a defensible range. Be prepared to produce your documentation if asked."[5]

After you've become clear about your desires and you are meeting with a representative of the organization, do not announce those desires when you first encounter the other person. "After you know what you want, the next step is to find out what the other person wants....Don't guess, and don't assume. ASK."[6] It is important to pay attention carefully before it is your turn to present your wants. "When you...arrive at the negotiating event, you must discipline yourself to practice effective listening techniques. If you are carefully concentrating on what's going on, you can learn a great deal about the other side's feelings, motivation, and real needs."[7]

If you listen first, you will have a better chance of being heard when you speak. "People listen better, sooner, and longer when you speak to their needs first...but...research shows that people speak first to the other person's needs only three percent of the time....We usually speak first to our own needs because we are unclear about what we want and are trying to figure it out as we talk, or because we're secretly afraid we can't have it and we are trying to trick, overwhelm, or fast-talk others into giving it to us. The result is that people close down and are less receptive to what we say."[8] You will be able to listen carefully if you have done your research and written down what you want before the negotiation begins.

If you are working with a recruiter, they will ask what your last year's salary was on your W2. If it is way over the range that the organization can offer, they won't present you as a candidate.[9]

An organization that is interviewing you for a physician executive position might offer you a salary of $200,000 and the standard benefits of health, life, dental, and disability insurance, retirement, vacation, and CME time. You might want some additional benefits, such as car allowance, relocation costs, or tuition for an MBA.

After you have listened carefully to the other person's needs, it is essential to let them know you have heard them. Here is a possible opening for your part of the negotiation after you have listened well: "I am really pleased that you want me for this position, and I think that I could accept your base salary and benefits, even though they are lower than what I had hoped for, if you could give me...."

Try to have some logic to support what you want. Don't ask for an automobile allowance unless you are traveling for the company. If you park your car in the office lot from 8 a.m. to 6 p.m., don't expect a car allowance. Ask for financial assistance with obtaining an MBA if you feel that would enhance your value to the organization. You could ask for moving expenses or a signing bonus as a way to enhance the initial package and allow the organization to keep the base salary in line with other executive salaries.

"A signing bonus is usually offered to make up for a bonus you are walking away from, unvested income that you are leaving, or a cost of living differential. Your ability to negotiate your salary and bonus will be based on how unique you are and how badly they need you. There are lots of good VPMAs and CMOs out there right now."[9]

"Train yourself to say, in every one of your negotiations, 'If everything goes wrong, will my life end?' If the answer to this question is no, teach yourself to say, 'Big deal, Who cares?' and 'So what?' Develop the attitude of caring but not caring that much."[10]

"Employment contracts are an option in some companies, but most will not offer them. It is worth it to ask for one, but even if it is not offered, make sure that you get all your agreements in writing in an offer letter. This is critical and can be just as legally binding as an employment contract."[11] "Our best advice is not to resign your present job until you have this written offer. Too many colleagues have been caught without any job at all because they failed to take this simple and reasonable step....Remember, you can negotiate a reasonable contract for yourself if you arm yourself with information and get it all in writing."[12]

Negotiation That Went Well

The following is an example of how a physician negotiated to get a job and then continued to use negotiation skills when he was in the medical director position:

"I left pediatric practice after being a clinician for 30 years. I went to work for Prudential PruCare. I was the 51st person they interviewed for a statewide medical director position. I told them I wasn't interested in the job, and I wanted to be the last one interviewed. I knew nothing about managed care.

"I had lunch with them. I was honest with them. I said, 'Number one, I am not running away from pediatric practice. I'm thinking of a second career. I'm moving to something better. I love pediatrics. I could spend the rest of my life in it and be happy. I am going to something. I'm not running away.' That's the first point that I got across. The second point was that I was always an innovator. I demonstrated how I had had a full-time pediatric practice and basically was only in the office three days a week.

"They asked me, 'How do you think you would do in this job after practicing for 30 years? Do you think you could discipline physicians and do what's necessary?' I said, 'My wife and sons know me better than I know myself. I'm going to go home and ask them if I can do it.' They said, 'You're the kind of person we are looking for-one who has an open mind,' and they handed me a contract.

"I think they wanted to take a chance on somebody who had different ideas. I stayed with them for five or six years. I learned a lot. That's when I got involved in ACPE, because when I took the job, I knew nothing about management skills.

"I was their first full-time medical director in the entire country. I wasn't sure I wanted to give up pediatric practice, so I negotiated staying in practice and working full time with Prudential. At the beginning when I went to work for Prudential, I was dying to get back to my practice, but, as the years went by, I was dying to get back to Prudential. Two and a half years later, I closed my office.

"My wife loves to read ads. She read about a job opening in western Massachusetts. She said, 'I want to go to a craft show out there, and there is a small HMO that is advertising for somebody. Why don't you set up an interview so you can drive out there with me.' It was a small HMO-five or six years old-that I wasn't really interested in, so I decided I would negotiate like heck. They offered me a salary that was one and a half times what I was making at Prudential. And I said, 'No, that's not nearly enough.' They said, 'That's the highest we can go.' So I said, 'That's a four-day-a-week salary. I'll only work four days a week.' They said, 'That's fine. You can take off every Friday.'

"I found a gorgeous new home, which is why I took the job. I never could have afforded it in the Boston area. I like to do crafts, and I have a 72-foot workshop in the basement. A magnificent home that in the Boston area would have been millions of dollars, and here it was much cheaper. I looked at the house, which has 44 windows, and I said I need money to put curtains on the windows. I negotiated for decorating costs. By then I figured I had a good deal.

"What I got as a bonus was that, because it was a young company, the senior management team had planned a supplementary retirement plan for themselves that was taxable at the end of the year but was based on average salary and the number of years until you were 65. They were getting 3 or 4 percent of their gross pay as a cash payment at the end of the year. This was in addition to their 401k. I came in at the age of 58 and had 7 years to retirement, so I get 20-25 percent of my total reimbursement each year as a cash payment.

"In negotiating a salary, if an organization wants somebody, they will be willing to pay. I never burned my bridges behind me. I always had a place to go back to, and I wasn't running away from my practice."

When I asked the physician how he learned to negotiate like that, he said, "I grew up in the depression. I was a street kid. My parents taught me if you don't ask you'll never get. The secret to negotiation to me is to make the interpersonal relationship with the people good and to give them what they want. You can't win anything by taking things away from people. You can win by giving things to people. This is how I got the doctors and everybody in the plan to be so productive. I never went in with a punitive attitude. I always went in with the attitude of giving them something extra, showing them why it would be in their best interest to do something rather than why it would be in their worst interest not to do something.

"I always negotiated by showing the person how they were getting the better part of the deal. In one of the doctor's offices, the secretaries at the end of the day would send patients to the emergency department instead of having them be seen by the doctor. This was a capitated plan so the emergency department got the money. Nothing for the office. Big problem.

"I did two things to solve this problem. I'm good with computers. I found out that a way I could identify when this was happening was by comparing the ratio of office visits to specialty referrals. If there were very few office visits and a lot of specialty referrals, I knew the secretary was doing this at the end of the day. I called up the secretaries and said, 'Don't you like big bonuses at the end of the year? Your doctor gets bonuses for money that is not spent, and the people who go to the emergency department cost money. The bonus will be less, and you will get less money at the end of the year.' They started to get the patients into the office earlier. That helped a little bit.

"Then I turned it around the other way in talking with the doctors. The average doctor with a panel of 300 patients has 300 emergency department visits a year. Let's say that's what the average doctor in a specialty does. I made patient age and gender adjustments so one doctor couldn't claim having a sicker panel of patients than others. I explained costs to the plan and to the doctors. 'What we will do is open an account for you and we'll credit you with $50 times 300 visits, or $15,000. Every time one of your patients goes to the emergency department, justified or unjustified, we'll deduct $50 from that account and at the end of the year you will get the balance that's left in it.' The doctors said to me, 'You're fining us $50 every time we see a patient.' I said, 'No, I'm giving you $15,000. You're spending your own money. How you spend it is up to you.' Emergency department referrals dropped 25 percent immediately, and they stayed down. The next year, we took the average number of referrals and established a $12,000 credit per doctor. It dropped to $9,000 the next year. We are spending less and less for emergency department referrals because each year we renegotiate the credit. And the doctors are tickled pink. A punitive negotiation has been turned into a very positive one that gives them an incentive to do something.

Negotiation That Did Not Go Well

The following is an example of a negotiation that did not go well. I think you will see that, in some situations, all the negotiation techniques in the world won't work, because the power rests with the other side.

"I work in a pediatric intensive unit in a general hospital. I have accomplished quite a bit for the unit—utilization census improved over the past two years from 700 annual admissions to more than 900 admissions. Physician revenues improved from $700,000 to more than $1 million dollars. I felt, from administrative as well as financial aspects, that I had done a good job and deserved an increase in salary. I get straight salary with a potential bonus if we collect beyond a certain figure. I outlined all my accomplishments for the past two years and sent them to the COO. I didn't hear from him for over a month, so I sent another memo reminding him.

"He outlined a financial arrangement that a consultant had recommended. There is a 10 percent reduction of my salary if I perform to the best of my ability. If I don't perform to the best of my ability, there is a 40 percent reduction.

"The same thing was done to me two years ago. It was an unpleasant negotiation. We were in turmoil. We had an incompetent physician that I insisted be fired. They didn't want to put themselves in a position where they would be sued by this physician. When they refused to get rid of her, I walked out. I got a position at another institution and worked for one day, and then they faxed me in my hotel and said, 'Whatever your requirements, we will meet them. Please come back.' I came back. They forced her to resign and gave her four months' severance. Twenty-four hours before my contract expired, I got everything I needed. However, at that time I was in the driver's seat.

"Now the COO thinks he's got me in his grip. Then, I was the only intensivist left to take care of patients in the ICU. Whatever I asked for, I got. Now it's the other way around. I've been able to recruit two intensivists whose contracts are not due to be renewed for another year. The COO is in the driver's seat. He can now force me to accept the terms that he wanted me to accept two years ago. I'm in a bind, because I've indicated I'm not interested in moving anywhere else. I am happy with the hospital, and I've accomplished quite a bit-increased nursing staff, increased beds. The unit serves as a model for other units in the hospital. I feel we are finally moving in the right direction, and I don't want to just throw everything away and move.

"I had not seriously looked anywhere else until last week. I think they feel I don't have any other alternatives, so I've started looking to see what's available. I've gotten them to verbally agree to extend the arrangement through July."

This situation was not resolved when I interviewed the physician. My guess is there will not be a positive outcome from the physician's point of view. There were bad feelings between the parties from a previous negotiation, and the hospital was not desperate for the physician's services this time. Another physician said, "It's a question of supply and demand. If you are one of a hundred people who are lining up for a job and everybody looks about the same, your negotiating position is a lot less than if there are a 100 people and you are much more highly qualified than the others. In my case, a new position was created, and I fit the bill very nicely, so I had the power on my side. If you are really in demand, you can almost name your price, but you can't be greedy. If, on a scale of 1 to 10, you are perceived to be a 7, and you think you should be paid as a 10, it's not going to work. If you say you deserve the world, you lose credibility."

Don't let the person you're negotiating with know you don't want to move. He or she needs to always think you have options.

"If the organization is in financial distress you can negotiate more, and you can certainly negotiate severance. If the position is risky—organization had four CEOs in five years—no candidate will take that without a two-year severance.

"Negotiate with the long term in mind. You plan to be there a long time. You want to come in with people feeling good about you. If you have negotiated down to the last penny, people aren't going to be feeling good. It is far more important to come into a warm environment where you look like a collaborative person who wants to play for the team than that you got every last dollar.

"But negotiate with catastrophe in mind. One of the things that will almost always be put in a contract if you ask for it is a change of control. If your hospital is acquired and your job is eliminated, you should get severance and be released from your restrictive covenant."[9]

Susan Cejka, Managing Partner of Grant Cooper & Associates, an executive search firm in St. Louis, MO, made a one-hour video lecture for ACPE in Spring 2005. A number of the quotations earlier in this chapter are from that lecture.[9] She gives details of salary, bonus, benefits, and relocation costs from the point of view of the candidate and the organization. What you actually make in salary is about half of what it costs the organization to hire you. This is a good reality check as you plan your negotiations. The video not only gives you good information, but it gets you mentally ready to have the negotiation conversations. I highly recommend watching it before your next negotiation.

References

1. Anderson, K. *Getting What You Want. How to Reach Agreement and Resolve Conflict Every Time.* New York, N.Y.: Plume Books, 1994, p. 5.

2. Kennedy, M. *Get the Job You Want and the Money You're Worth.* Tampa, Fla.: American College of Physician Executives, 1995, p. 27.

3. *Ibid.,* p. 31.

4. Buyse, M., and Falcao-Blumenfeld, P. "Negotiating Contracts." *Journal of the American Medical Women's Association* 46(3):75,76,82, May-June 1991.

5. Kennedy, M., *op. cit.*, p. 28.

6. Anderson, K., *op. cit.*, p. 13.

7. Cohen, H. *You Can Negotiate Anything*. Secaucus, N.J.: Lyle Stuart Books, p. 106.

8. Anderson, K., *op. cit.*, p. 21.

9. Cejka, S. "Negotiating a Contract and Closing the Deal." Tampa, Fla.: American College of Physician Executives, 2005.

10. Cohen, H., *op. cit.*, p. 88.

11. Buyse, M., and Falcao-Blumenfeld, P. *op. cit.* p. 75.

12. *Ibid.*, p. 82.

Work Sheet

Minimally acceptable salary   _____

Desired salary   _____

Required benefits   _____

_____

_____

_____

_____

_____

Desired benefits   _____

_____

_____

_____

_____

_____

Chapter Eleven

What To Do When Fired

Organizations are merging and holding their executives responsible for profits and losses. A new CEO comes in and wants to hire his/her own team. JACHO gives a less than stellar review, and the organization wants a scapegoat. These are some of the things that cause physician executives to lose their jobs. One recruiter says, "It is not a question of if you will be fired, but only a question of when." Most good, experienced physician executives he knows have been through it.

Hardworking, conscientious, charming, politically astute people are losing their jobs. How might you see it coming, and how can you cope with and move through the loss?

Here are some warning signs that you may be the victim of downsizing and some conditions that might increase your vulnerability[1]:

1. Others know you don't like what you do.

2. People stop listening to you. You are not included in meetings. You are not part of decision making.

3. You receive negative performance reviews.

4. You are not personally productive. You don't do anything new or creative.

5. You are failing to change; for instance, you are unwilling to learn to use new technology. People say that you refused to learn a new technique because you didn't agree with the change.

6. You aren't comfortable with a new culture.

7. You have poor communication skills—talk too much or too little.

8. You miss objectives set by you or your boss.

9. Economic conditions are negative. Census is going down. In a new organization created by acquisition or merger, only one CEO or medical director is needed.

10. You cost too much. Someone can be brought in at half the price to do the job.

"Because it's so traumatic, job loss is the third most severe loss people can suffer. In many ways, people's reactions to losing their jobs duplicate their reactions to the number one loss, death of a loved one, and the number two loss, divorce....Throughout the loss cycle, people report feeling a lack of control, increased stress, mounting anxiety, and moments of heart-stopping fear....Some people move quickly through the various stages after they have been laid off; others move slowly, taking as much as a year or more to complete the cycle; others move forward and then drop back to repeat a stage in a sort of two steps forward, one step back pattern.[2]

The following is a description of reactions people usually experience when they lose jobs. The list is not meant to imply that you must go through all these reactions in a prescribed order to get over the loss, but it is meant to remind you that, if you are experiencing some or all of these feelings, they are normal and expected. "If you know how people typically react to job loss, you can move more quickly through the stages that make it difficult to begin again."[3]

Shock

In this stage, occurring immediately after they are told they will be laid off, people are numb and unresponsive. They find it difficult to do anything, even to talk.

Denial

In this stage, a common reaction is disbelief. Some people, after they have been notified, race around trying to finish a project or a report as if they refuse to believe that their job has ended.

Anger

In this stage, people say things like, "They can't do this to me. I'll show them. I don't deserve this. Where's my lawyer?" Typically, men exhibit more anger than women do. They sometimes deny their feelings of depression, guilt, and grief. Women deny and internalize their anger, turning it into depression, guilt, and grief. People who get in touch with all these feelings move through the cycle more quickly.

Bargaining

In this stage, people fantasize about steps they could have taken in the past to avoid being laid off. Round and round they go in their minds, like a hamster running a wheel.

Guilt

In this stage, people blame themselves for the loss of job. They are ashamed. They revisit in their minds every lapse or failure or rejection in their lives. The disappointments and hurts of a lifetime come rushing back into their minds.

Depression

In this stage, people question their value. "I'm no good. It's no wonder they don't want me." They gain or lose weight, sleep too much or too little, hide away, and hit bottom.

Grief

In this stage, people reflect on what they have lost and are sad. They mourn the loss. Even if they didn't love their jobs, they mourn the loss of the familiar.

Acceptance

In this stage, people begin to "get on with it." They say, "There's nothing I can do about it." They feel excitement about the future.

Involvement and Commitment

In this stage, people are ready to become involved with a new organization and to make a commitment to that organization, although it is often a different kind of work commitment than they have ever made in the past. They recognize that the greater your investment in your job, the more devastating it is to lose. They vow in the future to maintain a better balance between work and the rest of their lives."[4]

The following suggestions can sometimes help you move through the stages more quickly:

- "Keep a journal. A private log of your thoughts and feelings can help you get in touch with and sort through your emotions. Research indicates that people who keep journals not only move through the stages more quickly, but also find reemployment more quickly."[3]

- Tell your spouse. Even though your spouse will also be going through the loss cycle, you will both move through it more quickly if your spouse is not blaming and resentful.

- Talk to a friend about the emotional ups and downs. It is especially helpful if you can talk to people who have been through the experience.

- Talk to a professional counselor.

Two Real-Life Experiences

Following are interviews with two physician executives who experienced job loss. Details have been altered to protect the identity of the interviewees.

First Physician Executive

What position did you have?

I was Chief Medical Officer of a large tertiary hospital in the Northwest. I had been there a little over 2 years. This hospital had a high number of Medicare patients, and it was hit hard by DRGs, the first wave of managed care to hit hospitals. One of my roles was change agent to influence physician practice patterns. We turned around a lot of the cost problems by looking at physician behavior.

The CEO who hired me retired, and a new CEO was brought in. He pulled a group of senior managers together and we went on a two-day retreat. The word was, "You are the group I'm keeping." During my entire tenure, the medical director whom I had been hired to replace never left the premises. The role that he had developed for himself never evolved, and there was no funding for it.

How did it happen?

I was informed that I had been terminated by letter, which the CEO's secretary brought into me about 4:00 one Friday afternoon. This was less than three weeks after the retreat where I was told I was part of the team. This was not too long after I had received a raise, all sorts of commendations, certain financial securities, and parachutes as a reward for a job well done. I was on top of the world, and yet, within no more than four-six weeks, my world came tumbling down. The letter said, "We have one too many physician managers. You've done a good job, but you are the last in and the first out. We can't afford three, and we need two."

I managed to leave the office with my head held high. I thought my world had collapsed. I came home that afternoon and my wife said, "What are you doing home so early?" I never came home at 4:00. I usually came home at 6:00 or 7:00. I sat down on the edge of the chair and I said, "I've lost faith in humanity," and I cried. I don't cry very often, but I cried. To my wife's credit, after a few minutes she picked me up and said, "Go clean up. We're going out, have a dinner, and celebrate the move to the next stage of the rest of our lives."

I forced the CEO to write to the medical staff exactly what had happened. I didn't want to have to explain it to everybody. I knew it would get out, and I wanted the CEO to go up front and explain what happened and why. I also jumped all over him for the way he did it. He needed to have the guts to look me in the eye. I told him I respected the fact that he was paid to make hard decisions. Although I didn't agree with his decision, I respected his right to make that decision. It was just handed to me the wrong way.

What was the worst part of being fired?

The worst part was the abject shock. I knew there were some warning signs—the other fellow never left, a new CEO came in, the CEO and the previous medical director had been friends—and yet I felt fairly secure, mainly because of the rewards I had received, the validation at the retreat, the parachute that was given to me for a job well done. I was still blindsided, and the pain of that time and the pain of the next few days and the humiliation of telling my family and friends was probably the most difficult thing I've ever gone through in my life.

As you look back at your firing, was there a good part to it for your life and for your future?

Yes. It forces you to take stock, use this time to pause and rethink where you are in your career and where you want to be. It validates the fact that you can pick yourself up off the floor and you can wipe the blood off your nose and you can climb up and achieve things that you may not have gotten before through the support of friends and family and network and just digging down deep into yourself. I think the measure of a person is how they respond to adversity. As painful as it is, it tests you. I probably have a greater feeling of self-worth now that I've picked myself up. I had a family that stood by me, a network that stood by me. I had more opportunities than you can shake a stick at. I'm a whole lot smarter. I couldn't say the "f" word for a while. Now I can tell people I was fired. I don't have to tell them I was terminated, or I would explain the situation and not say the word. It is one of those words that sounds like what it is. I think that is called onomatopoeia. "Fired" is a harsh, cutting word.

How long did it take to feel better?

I think it took two-four weeks. [We were talking on the phone, and he called to his wife in another room and said, "How long did it take me before I was out of a funk?" She called back, "Four and closer to eight weeks."] For a while, you just beat yourself up.

What helped you?

The first week I called a friend and a professional career counselor whose business it is to counsel and advise people at a time like this. I kept a diary at his recommendation. I wouldn't have done it on my own. I still haven't looked at it. It's here. When we make explicit what was implicit, it has a different meaning. It's like when you are forced to write down your goals and put them on paper, it has a different meaning than if you just think them. The exercise of going through that had a bit of a healing effect, purging yourself of the demons. I recommend that you seek professional advice and don't be too proud to do that and think that you know everything about everything.

I made a business of resurrecting my career and moving forward. Each morning I got dressed, went into the office in my home, and went to work. I kept a calendar, I had hours and I had appointments. I just started turning over stones. Fortunately, I had kept my resume with most of the physician executive headhunters. I called some key people in the American College of Physician Executives.

I went to work for a consulting firm in three months. That offer had been on the table before. I had copresented with this consulting firm because our hospital was used as a model for how to lower costs by changing physician practice patterns. It always said to me anytime you want to work with us, call us. Plus, I had had the usual bevy of calls we all receive at work, as most of the headhunters are looking for somebody who already has a job, not somebody who doesn't have a job.

Are there things you wish you had or hadn't done?

I've thought about it a 100 million times. At times, I don't think so. I was proud of the job I did. At other times, I've thought I could have been more politically adroit. I could have spent more time with some of the key power players of the hospital.

Are there lessons you have learned?

One of the things I've learned is that we need to take responsibility for all that happens to us. Any time there's failure or something doesn't work out, you have to assume it wasn't all just circumstances. Perhaps there were some things you could have done better, some things you didn't do, or politically you could have been more astute.

Sure there is a political piece to it. The guy in the background came back in and did my job. I was a change agent. I wasn't a caretaker medical director. I had not grown up in that hospital. I didn't have the long history.

Unfortunately, it has made me more skeptical. By nature, I believe in humanity, and I like to have faith and trust in other human beings. This episode has made me a little bit jaded, and I think that is probably wise from a business perspective. I don't like it from a humanitarian perspective, because I tend to believe in the good in people and then they have to prove me wrong. I've become more cynical since then, but I've also come to realize that business is business and if possible try not even to personalize it, because it wasn't personal.

Also, I learned that, as long as you are working for somebody else, there is no absolute security—that no matter what is said or written down, there is no absolute security; that changes take place in organizations at lots of different levels all the time; that when you work for someone you are a commodity; and that a lot of times, when a new CEO comes in, he or she makes a lot of changes, right or wrong, good or bad.

Does anything else come to mind?

I've got great things to say about ACPE, because, without the College, I probably never would have gotten some of those positions. I think one of the undervalued parts of the College is the network and the fact that every time I have called anybody and asked for advice and counsel, there was just an outpouring of help from everybody. I don't know if it is underutilized, but I didn't appreciate the power of the organization until I went through that and I'll be forever grateful. That is one of the reasons why I'm so involved and why I'm trying to give back, because I don't know what I would have done without an anchor. I guess I would have survived, but it sure made it a lot easier. We all need anchors in the storm. Word leaked out. People in the College called and said, "Have you considered this? Have you considered that?"

What advice would you give to others in the same situation?

You have to prepare as if it is going to happen. You have to have everything in place as if you could get fired tomorrow. Never, never, never assume that it can't happen to you or that it won't happen to you. If you chronicle most successful business people in life, many of them have had a similar experience somewhere along the way, whether it was in early, middle, or senior management.

Being fired is like being smacked with a whip. You go into your office one day, and, "blam," it happens, and your whole world collapses. Is everything in place? Do you have a network? Do they understand what you do? Is your resume current? Have you kept yourself in visible positions by writing or speaking or taking leadership roles in the organization? Preparation ahead of time is essential.

Also, take the high road. You don't point fingers. You don't blame what happened on any-one else. In fact, you don't have to blame it on anyone. It's just that certain things happen. You accept your fate. I watched my favorite pro basketball team last night, and they just got shellacked. Some days you just get shellacked, and you just keep your mouth shut and move ahead. Many people get fired, but when you blame other people, you hurt yourself. You're not going to hurt the organization. Sooner or later, it will come back and just kill you.

Second Physician Executive

(At the time of the interview, three months had passed since this physician executive had been fired.)

What position did you have?

I was Vice President for Medical Affairs at a large general hospital.

How did the downsizing happen?

The hospital started eliminating positions over the past two years. It eliminated more than 30 positions, and one of them was the VPMA. Morale was awful. I had been participating in the top management team and selecting people to let go, little realizing that I would be selected. I got 24 hours' notice. The hospital said my firing would be announced the next day. There was a brief discussion, and I said, "I think you are making a mistake."

Can you see any good part it has for you and your career?

There may be. For one thing, I've been in this a long time. Economically, it is no problem, which is fortunate. I can see how someone could really get in difficulty if there is an eco-nomic problem.

Did you have a severance package already in place?

Yes. That was in the contract, and I think that is absolutely critical. I wouldn't take a job without it. Basically what is happening is that you essentially work at will. Almost all con-tracts have a termination clause, so you have to protect yourself. Reductions in force are occurring everywhere. As I talk around, there are a number of VPMAs who have been reduced out of their jobs, so you really have to prepare for it. There is an inherent tension between an administrator and a VPMA, because, as they move into the whole cost versus quality issue, most administrators have no knowledge of quality, but they have the assumption that they know what they are doing. As administrators come under increasing pressure, they resent physicians in general and firing them makes a nice scapegoating. These things are going to probably get worse. I think traditional administrators fear they are going to be replaced by physician administrators. So there is more hostility and attempts to get them out of the environment.

Did you feel the initial numbness of shock and devastation or, because you had a good severance package, did you pretty much take it in stride?

Well, it really knocks you off your feet, whether you have a severance package or not.

How long did it take you to regain your equilibrium, or have you?

I think I've pretty well gained that. I got a lot of support. I got support, surprisingly, from the medical staff, even from people with whom I had raised major issues. That support was pleasant and surprising. I've had support from my family. Also from other physicians in ACPE. People called me, and I called them. I started to network. I'm going out tomorrow to look into some sort of thing in terms of consulting.

What helped?

The announcement appeared in the newspaper the next day. A subspecialist called me up and said he wanted to work out a position for me. He thought I had talent that would be useful in putting together an organization.

Are there lessons you have learned?

One of the key things that I see was that I was recruited in by an administrator who subsequently left. When there is a change of administrators, there is a time of testing. That person coming in has little knowledge of what you have done and may have a preconceived picture of the position. The person may well have had problems with physicians in the past and bring those prejudices to bear on you.

Do you have any advice to others?

Yes. It is devastating to get fired. You probably ought to sit back and look at what you want to do in the future. Then start to network with people. I started networking right away. I set up a home office.

It is very important to have support early on. I didn't want to move geographically, so that immediately limited my choices. But I'm a very senior person. I wouldn't have kept working too much longer anyhow. I've talked to other people who are much younger, and it took them up to a year to find something. It's a different situation for me, because I'm not looking for that sort of thing. It's important to talk to people you have worked with in the past in other management positions and try to establish a connection there.

It is absolutely critical to get a good attorney, particularly if you can get someone who is knowledgeable about hospitals. If you are older, the firing organization will try to say that you are retired, but it is important to get it to say in any agreement that it was a reduction of force, not retirement, because then a restrictive covenant doesn't hold. If you are recruited into a hospital, most contracts say you can't take another similar position within so many miles within a year or two after you quit. That would hold if you retired. As a result of using an attorney, I was able to negotiate very favorable terms. That's important, on top of whatever sort of parachute you have. I had a couple of months to work this out.

How did you hear about that person?

I talked to an attorney that I had worked with and asked who would you recommend?

Conclusion

Firing seems like a devastating event, even if recruiters call you fairly regularly about other possibilities. The rejection feels personal, and it takes some time to get over the initial shock. The support of a well-developed network of professional contacts, family, and friends softens the blow. After a short period of grieving, it is important to get busy and contact people in order to move to the next phase of your career.

References

1. Tiffan, W. "When Downsizing Points to You." Presentation at ACPE Perspectives in Medical Management, Chicago, Ill., May 1995.

2. Baber, A., and Waymon, L. *How to Fireproof Your Career. Survival Strategies for Volatile Times.* New York, N.Y.: Berkley Books, 1995.

3. *Ibid.,* p. 80.

4. *Ibid.,* pp. 77-9.

Chapter Twelve

Helpful Tools for the Job Search — Ways to Keep Your Sanity

In Chapter 11, a physician executive mentioned the benefits of keeping a journal if you are fired. A journal can be a useful tool throughout the job search. You can keep track of the daily tasks necessary to pursue a new position, give concrete formation to your goals, and change the thoughts in your head from negative to positive to keep an essential optimistic outlook for finding a job. Keeping a journal can also help you cope with the stresses of your present job. Many have reported that the reflective time required by writing helps them to make sense of and find meaning in their lives.

Journal

I suggest that you write in a journal 10 minutes a day, 5 days week. A journal is whatever kind of paper you like. I like wide-ruled, thick, five-subject spiral notebooks with white paper and blue lines. Maybe you like yellow legal paper, although most doctors I know don't. You can type on your word processor if that suits you better but not on your computer at the office or in your email system.

I write with cheap pens of which I have an unlimited supply. When I've used an expensive pen, I spend all my time worrying about when I'll lose the pen rather than thinking about what I am writing. If you like an expensive pen, buy one, buy two. The point is—be specific about your likes and dislikes and pamper yourself as much as possible. Write in your favorite spot with all the utensils, accompaniments, and frills that please you. Cater to your slightest whim. You don't need to discipline yourself about what materials you use or where you write. A large part of getting yourself to write in a journal is getting over whatever kind of discipline or even abuse you suffered at the hand of some teacher during your education process. If ever your paper was snatched from you and read to the whole class, you probably have significant paralysis to overcome.

In this journal that you have carefully chosen, do a special kind of writing called freewriting. When you freewrite, you write whatever comes into your mind. You don't worry about spelling, punctuation, grammar, or anything that some English teacher told you to always worry about. "There are no fixed rules for journal writing....It's not a place to condemn nor judge, but a place to observe. Pay no attention at all to your 'style' of writing."[1] Your handwriting or typing does not have to be neat or accurate. No one will see anything you write.

There is only one catch. For the process to work well, you need to keep writing until the 10 minutes are up. Set a timer if you have to. I know that two pages of nonstop writing in my spiral notebook always equals ten minutes. If you can't think of anything to write, just say over and over, " I can't think of anything to write. I can't think of anything to write. I wonder when I will think of something." But keep moving your pen and writing something, even if it is nonsense. There is a reason for this. Ideas will pop into your head if you keep writing that won't come if you just sit thinking.

Keep this freewriting private. If you momentarily hate your boss, it's good to write about it. It is not good for him or her to see it. If you write something that would be especially dangerous for someone to see, tear it up when you finish. You'll probably discover that writing takes you places you didn't know you were going to go. You'll begin writing about one idea, and then, suddenly, some other thought pops into your head. Write it down. Don't discipline yourself to stay on a particular subject. Your very best ideas may come trailing after the strangest thoughts.

Marion describes the journal specifically for the pursuit of a job: "Your career search journal is an important way to track your physical and emotional progress, to hear what you have to say to yourself. Record doubts, ideas, impressions, anything interesting that happened that you might want to remember."[2] Leider describes it in broader terms: "When you write in a journal, you're not composing an essay, only recording the unedited expressions of your inner experience. You write in it day by day as much as possible to keep yourself in an ongoing relationship with whatever is taking place inside yourself....Journaling helps you observe your inner conversation more objectively....A journal is a mirror. It's a good listener, a tool for self-guidance, a road map of growth....Some never go back to read in their journals. Others reread continuously to get a feeling of trends in their life."[3] You decide which is helpful for you.

The hottest new trend in the job search world is thousands of job postings on the internet site, monster.com. The founder, Jeff Taylor, in his book *Monster Careers*, still speaks to the power of writing. "I've drawn from the latest thinking about self-assessment and innovative ways to help you gain insights about yourself." He has eight writing exercises at the end of the chapter called, "Who Are You." He then adds, "As you develop more insights about what you like and dislike, write them down...."[4] The speed of "point and click" in the information age has not changed the value of writing to discover what you think and feel.

As I have mentioned, I am the spouse of a physician executive. A journal can be beneficial to the spouse as well as to the physician executives. I keep a journal except when I forget to. I can forget for a month at a time. Even though I teach the concept and know it is helpful, I still have lapses of not doing it. I want you to know I know how difficult it will be to get yourself to do this. However, it is worth the effort.

We have made two geographic moves. I did not want to make the first move. I did want to make the second one, but the stresses of moving were great, even though I felt I was going home again. Following is a journal entry during the stressful time of moving. I let you see movies of my mind to see how incoherent, rambling, and confusing a journal entry can be.

Sample of journal entry during a job change and move

Friday I am doing a program in Cape Cod. I speak from 8-12 with an hour for lunch and then speak from 1-4. At noon someone hands me a note saying—They are having trouble with your house closing. Adrenaline rushes. I call the law office. Earlier in the week we had signed a power of attorney to a lawyer so he could do the closing for us. He had transferred the money we were borrowing from the bank to the closing destination. However, I did not remember and the realtor did not remind me to transfer the cash money from the sale of our Orlando house to the closing. Mercifully I had wired that money to a NC bank. I didn't have with me the phone numbers of the 2 people from the NC bank that had processed our loan and had opened the account where that money sat. With 4 phone calls it was worked out but once again I am trying to calm myself.

Use a Journal to Write Goals

Dr. Lee Pulos did research that showed only 4 percent of the population write down their goals. However, those who do write down their goals achieve them almost 100 percent of the time.[5] "You need to have a clear picture of what you want, with no inner conflict about whether you deserve it or not."[6] "To be successful you have to believe that you deserve success. You have to have an image of yourself so tangible that you can reach out and touch it."[7]

Writing in your journal is a way to make the goal tangible. If you write out a goal, your brain thinks it, your hand writes it, your eyes see it clearly on the paper, and your subconscious and the universe plan ways to make it happen. "Setting down your plans on paper takes you a step further than just deciding on a career goal and talking about it with others. It constitutes a deeper commitment to yourself. Also, seeing it on paper makes it more concrete."[8] If you keep your goals where you can see them each day, you can determine if you are truly spending your time trying to accomplish them or if you value other things more. If the latter, be honest with yourself and change your goals.

If I am overwhelmed with too many tasks and think I'm a bit off track, I will pick up my journal and write the answers to these questions:

- Is this what I want to be doing?

- Does this move me toward my goal?

- What is that nagging irritation?

- Can I do anything about it now? If not, I write it down so I don't use energy trying to remember it or trying to forget it. I can deal with it later and get back to working on my goal.

Make a list of your goals—things you want to do or accomplish. Make it long, imaginative, demanding of yourself. "One of the most interesting immediate results of writing your goals down clearly, concisely, and without ambiguity, and then memorizing them, is that you will feel better when you have done so. The reason for this is that...you are doing something your biocomputer has been wanting you to do. It is as though the biocomputer heaves a great sigh of relief and says, 'At last. Now I know where we are going.'"[9]

Self-Talk

A journal is also a place to observe your self-talk—the kind of thinking that goes on in your head all day long. If you see what self-talk is going on in your head, you can change it. "People who are optimistic tend to find jobs faster. They have more energy and follow up on leads. They tell themselves positive things."[10] "If you fail to control your own thoughts, you will have difficulty controlling anything else."[11] Charles Garfield suggests that, if you can visualize a positive outcome and say self-assuring things to yourself, you greatly increase the chances of reaching your goal.[12] While writing, you see your own negative self-talk and empty it onto the page. Then you can replace it with positive thoughts.

When you write a negative thought, you'll know that's the program your brain computer is running. You have to install a different program using a quite specific method. The new program can be a positive thought about behavior or a picture in your head of a goal you want to achieve. "If you want the new program to be a permanent part of your subconscious, you have to repeat it to yourself under two very specific conditions, 12-15 times a day for 14 or more days (i.e., about 200 repetitions.)"[13] The more the better. Every time the negative program starts in your head, substitute the new one. That worry and negative thought can be a reminder to do the repetitions.

"If you trigger a relaxation response before you do the rehearsal, the new positive thoughts tend to be absorbed much more quickly."[14] "If you become exhausted, highly emotional, or under the influence of alcohol or other drugs and the old stimulus occurs, the brain may very well go to the old response. You can't do anything about that, except try not to be in those situations. The more you rehearse, the less likely a reversion is, but the old program is always there and may play from time to time."[15]

Leider describes this process as visualization. "Visualization means talking to yourself silently in a soft but firm tone....Deep prayer, biofeedback, meditation, positive thinking all begin with visualization. It's all a matter of getting yourself into a receptive state."[16] Peter Senge, in *The Fifth Discipline*, describes how some form of meditation helps people excel. "[P]eople committed to continually developing personal mastery practice some form of 'meditation.' Whether it is through contemplative prayer or other methods of simply 'quieting' the conscious mind, regular meditative practice can be extremely helpful in working more productively with the subconscious mind....In our normal highly active state of mind, the subconscious is deluged with a welter of contradictory thoughts and feelings. In a quieter state of mind, when we focus on something of particular importance, some aspect of our vision, the subconscious is undistracted....[D]uring that time) people with high levels of personal mastery direct their focus....[T]hey focus on the desired result itself, not the 'process' or the means they assume necessary to achieve that result."[17]

"Since visualizations only have a life-span of about 36 hours, you'll need to repeat this process daily, until you've truly changed your behavior or reached your goal."[18] "[S]etting aside time for visualizations each day is like an artist's brushstroke toward the completion of the painting."[19]

Dr. Lee Pulos claims we say between 45,000 and 51,000 words to ourselves each day.[5] Only an experienced meditator can go for 11 seconds without self-talk. For a lot of people, much of what they are saying to themselves has a doomsday theme to it.

"You participate in a daily dialogue—everything you say to yourself and others during the day—all thoughts both deliberate and spontaneous. Your dialogue is so important because it is the way you give instructions to yourself—both to your body and to your mind. It is important to change your dialogue to yourself and others from negative, self-destructive things to positive self-enhancing things.

"You are what you tell yourself you are. You feel what you tell yourself you feel. You become what you tell yourself. It doesn't matter whether or not you actually believe the new dialogue. In fact, it will not be true in the beginning, and it will feel strange and uncomfortable. The essence of change is to do something enough until it becomes true."[20]

The repetition of positive statements may strike you as contrived and too easy. If you try it, you'll find it takes quite a bit of discipline to control the thoughts in your head, but it can be done. You may think your positive statement is a lie. That doesn't matter—say it to yourself anyway. It will become the truth.

The use of a journal and positive self-talk will spur you on to do the work necessary to find your next job and enhance your career.

References

1. Leider, R. *Life Skills*. San Diego, Calif.: Pfeiffer & Company, 1994, p. 184.

2. Marion, P. *Crisis Proof Your Career*. New York, N.Y.: Berkley Books, 1994, p. 172.

3. Leider, R., *op cit.*, pp. 183-4.

4. Taylor, J. *Monster Careers*, New York, N.Y.: Penguin Books, 2004, p. 73.

5. Pulos, L.. "The Power of Visualization." An audiotape series produced by Nightingale-Conant Corporation, 7300 N. Lehigh Ave., Niles, Ill. 60714, 800/323-5552.

6. Marion, P. *op. cit.*, p. 31.

7. *Ibid.*, p. 97.

8. *Ibid.*, p. 141.

9. Thomas, P. *Advanced Psycho-Cybernetics*. New York, N.Y.: Perigee Books, 1992, p. 128.

10. Marion, P., *op. cit.*, p. 33.

11. Thomas, P., *op. cit.*, p. 182.

12. Garfield, C. *Top Performers: The New Heroes of American Business*. New York, N.Y.: Avon Books, 1986.

13. Dwyer, C. *The Shifting Sources of Power and Influence*. Tampa, Fla.: American College of Physician Executives, 1991, p. 52.

14. Dwyer, C., *op. cit.*, p. 53.

15. *Ibid.*, p. 55.

16. Leider, R., *op. cit.*, p. 180.

17. Senge, P. *The Fifth Discipline*. New York, N.Y.: Doubleday Currency, 1990, p. 164.

18. Leider, R., *op. cit.*, p. 183.

19. Marion, P., *op. cit.*, p. 119.

20. Covington, F., and Seagrave, A. *CHAANGE Handbook*. Charlotte, N.C.: CHAANGE, 1986, p.9.

Other Reading

Alexander, J. *Dare to Change*. New York, N.Y.: A Signet Book, New American Library, 1984.

Baber, A., and Waymon, L. *How to Fireproof Your Career. Survival Strategies for Volatile Times*. New York, N.Y.: Berkley Books, 1995.

Covey, S. *The 7 Habits of Highly Effective People*. New York, N.Y.: Simon and Schuster, 1989.

Elbow, Peter. *Writing Without Teachers*. London, England: Oxford University Press, 1973.

Gillett, R. *Change Your Mind. Change Your World*. New York, N.Y.: Simon and Schuster, 1992.

Richardson, Cheryl. *The Unmistakable Touch of Grace*. New York: Free Press, 2005.

Wallen, E. "Job Pressures Seen Fueling Rise in Doctors' Stress Levels." *Physicians Financial News*, Oct. 15, 1993, pp. 15-6.

Wheelis, A. *How People Change*. New York, N.Y.: Harper Colophon Books, 1973.